# GRAMMAR AND BEYOND

## WORKBOOK

Kathryn O'Dell

# 3

CAMBRIDGE
UNIVERSITY PRESS

CAMBRIDGE UNIVERSITY PRESS
Cambridge, New York, Melbourne, Madrid, Cape Town,
Singapore, São Paulo, Delhi, Tokyo, Mexico City

Cambridge University Press
32 Avenue of the Americas, New York, NY 10013-2473, USA

www.cambridge.org
Information on this title: www.cambridge.org/9781107601970

First published 2012

Printed in the United States of America

*A catalog record for this publication is available from the British Library.*

ISBN 978-0-521-14298-4   Student's Book 3
ISBN 978-0-521-14315-8   Student's Book 3A
ISBN 978-0-521-14319-6   Student's Book 3B
ISBN 978-1-107-60197-0   Workbook 3
ISBN 978-1-107-60198-7   Workbook 3A
ISBN 978-1-107-60199-4   Workbook 3B
ISBN 978-1-107-68502-4   Teacher Support Resource Book with CD-ROM 3
ISBN 978-0-521-14339-4   Class Audio CD 3
ISBN 978-1-139-06187-2   Writing Skills Interactive 3

Cambridge University Press has no responsibility for the persistence or
accuracy of URLs for external or third-party Internet Web sites referred to in
this publication and does not guarantee that any content on such Web sites is,
or will remain, accurate or appropriate. Information regarding prices, travel
timetables, and other factual information given in this work is correct at
the time of first printing, but Cambridge University Press does not guarantee
the accuracy of such information thereafter.

Art direction and layout services: Integra

# Contents

# PART 3 The Future

# PART 4 Modals and Modal-like Expressions

# PART 7 Questions and Noun Clauses

# PART 8 Indirect Speech

# Art Credits

## Illustration

**Bill Dickson:** 29, 103, 204; **Ortelius Design:** 152; **Rob Schuster:** 11, 127 *(top)*, 195, 196, 202, 210, 221; **Matt Stevens:** 14, 26, 28, 34, 127 *(bottom)*, 128; **Richard Williams:** 19, 20, 186

## Photography

2 ©Photodisc/Thinkstock; 5 *(t)* ©iStockphoto/Thinkstock; *(b)* ©iStockphoto/Thinkstock; 12 Weegee(Arthur Fellig)/International Center of Photography / Getty Images; 21 Marc Romanelli/Getty Images; 37 ©Lisa F. Young/Alamy; 48 ©Jack Hollingsworth/Photodisc/Thinkstock; 52 ©Leila Cutler/Alamy; 59 ©iStockphoto/Thinkstock; 80 *(l)* ©Andrew Twort / Alamy; *(r)* Rob Melnychuk/Digital Vision/Getty Images; 82 ©Photos.com/Thinkstock; 85 ©PETER DASILVA/Redux; 86 Gilles Mingasson/Getty Images; 94 ©iStockphoto.com/Bariscan Celik; 100 ©iStockphoto.com/Michael Bodmann; 110 ©Mary Evans/Everett Collection; 132 Andersen Ross/Blend Images/Getty Images; 142 Leland Bobbe/Stone /Getty Images; 150 ©Hemera/Thinkstock; 168 ©MONPIX/Alamy; 170 Yuji Kotani/The Image Bank/Getty Images; 176 ©Pablo Paul/Alamy; 177 ©Hemera/Thinkstock; 180 ©Fox Searchlight/Everett Collection; 222 Jonas Ingerstedt/Johner Images/Getty Images; 228 ©New Line Productions/Zuma Press

# Simple Present and Present Progressive

## First Impressions

---

## Simple Present vs. Present Progressive

**1** Complete the article with the words in parentheses. Use the simple present or present progressive. Sometimes more than one answer is possible.

### Teacher of the Year

This month in our newsletter we <u>*are profiling*</u> (profile)
(1)
different teachers at Summerville Community College. Kevin

Lewis, a grammar teacher, was recently voted "Teacher of the

Year" here at Summerville. We interviewed some of the students

who voted for him to find out the reasons they think he is a really

effective teacher. Here are some of the things they said. "Mr. Lewis _____
(2)
(treat) all students fairly. He _____ (explain) everything carefully. He
(3)
_____ (not lose) his patience. This week, during exams, he
(4)
_____ (keep) extended office hours to help the students who need
(5)
extra help. He _____ (always / tell) students to feel free to
(6)
drop in to talk with him when they _____ (see) him in his office. He
(7)
_____ (always / make) a good impression on the first day of
(8)
class by dressing nicely, speaking clearly, and learning all the students' names. Mr. Lewis

respects the students, and we _____ (respect) him."
(9)

We also interviewed Mr. Lewis. Here are some of the things he had to say. "I

really like teaching. I _____ (wake up) every morning excited about
(10)
my classes. I _____ (teach) several classes this semester, but I
(11)
_____ (always / try) to be available for my students during
(12)
class and outside the classroom, too. Also, I think it's important to keep my students

motivated, so I _____ (constantly / look) for ways to make my
(13)
classes more interesting and enjoyable."

**2** Complete the sentences about a professor's research study. Use the words in parentheses with the simple present or present progressive.

1. Dr. Andrei Baronova _is_ (be) a professor of psychology.

2. He _____ (not teach) classes this semester.

3. Instead, he _____ (do) research on stress.

4. Specifically, he _____ (investigate) "test anxiety."

5. Some of his students from last semester _____ (participate) in
   this research, but others _____ (not work) with him.

6. He _____ (typically / meet) with these students once a week.

7. They _____ (often / talk) about their feelings during exams.

8. Dr. Baronova _____ (usually / ask) them specific questions.

9. At the moment, he _____ (ask) them questions about
   their "self-talk"[1] during exams because he believes that a lot of students
   _____ (generally / say) negative things to themselves.

10. At the same time, he _____ (also / teach) them how to use
    *positive* self-talk, not negative self-talk.

   ----
   [1]**self-talk:** what people say to themselves, for example, "I can't do this" (negative) and "I can do this" (positive)

**3** Complete the telephone conversation. Use the simple present or present progressive with the words in parentheses. Use contractions when possible.

**Kazuki:** Hi, Meena? It's Kazuki. What _are you doing_ (do)?
                                      (1)

**Meena:** Hi, Kazuki. I _____ (walk) to class. How about you?
                              (2)

**Kazuki:** Oh, I _____ (study) right now, but I'll need to relax later.
                     (3)
   _____ you _____ (want) to go to the movies
            (4)                              (4)
   tonight?

**Meena:** _____ the new Daniel Craig and Rooney Mara movie still
                  (5)
   _____ (play)?
            (5)

**Kazuki:** No. It _____ (not play) at the local theater anymore, but
                        (6)
   they _____ (show) *First and Last Impressions*.
               (7)

**Meena:** Oh, I _____ (want) to see that. What time does it start?
                      (8)

**Kazuki:** It _____ (start) at 6:15. Let's meet there at 6:00.
                    (9)

**Meena:** Great! See you then.

# Stative Verbs

**1** Greg is going to meet the parents of Rachel, the woman he is going to marry. Circle the correct forms of the verbs to complete the conversation. Remember that some verbs, such as *be*, *think*, and *have*, can have stative or action meanings.

**Alex:** Greg, are you nervous about meeting your fiancée's parents tonight?

**Greg:** Very! Rachel **says** / **is saying** they're great people, but right now **I have** / **I'm having**
(1)                                                                      (2)
trouble remembering that because I'm so nervous. My hands are shaking.

**Alex:** Really? You **don't seem** / **aren't seeming** nervous.
(3)

**Greg:** Well, I'm glad **I look** / **I'm looking** fine, anyway.
(4)

**Alex:** **Do you think** / **Are you thinking** about how to make a good first impression?
(5)

**Greg:** Yeah.

**Alex:** You **don't have** / **aren't having** anything to worry about. You need to relax!
(6)

**Greg:** Thanks. I'm sure you're probably right. I guess **I'm** / **I'm being** silly. Hey,
(7)
**do you hear** / **are you hearing** something? I think they're here!
(8)

**Alex:** Relax. It's not a job interview. They're probably nervous, too.

**Greg:** Well, **it feels** / **it's feeling** like a stressful interview for a really important job!
(9)
**I really want** / **I'm really wanting** to make a good first impression.
(10)

**Alex:** Well, I guess **I need** / **I'm needing** to go now! **I don't think** / **I'm not thinking**
(11)                                                    (12)
I should be here when you meet them. Good luck!

**2** Complete each pair of sentences with the simple present and present progressive forms of the same verb. Use the words in bold. In one sentence, the verb has a stative meaning. In the other sentence, the same verb has an action meaning.

**be** Jeff _is_ in a new town and doesn't know many people yet. This month he
(1)

_____ adventurous and trying an online dating service.
(2)

**have** He knows that some people who use online

dating websites _____ good
(3)

luck. Right now he _____ only
(4)

bad luck . . .

**see** Maybe the problem is that he always

_____ the imperfections in
(5)

people, so it's hard for him to find a good

match. At the moment, he _____ a woman he met at the grocery store.
(6)

**think** Jeff _____ about joining a hiking club, too. He _____ that
(7) (8)

might be a good way to meet new people, make friends, and get some exercise, too.

# Special Meanings and Uses of Simple Present

**1** Complete the article about "love at first sight." Use the simple present of the verbs in parentheses.

_Do_ you _believe_ (believe) in love at first sight?
(1) (1)

Some people _____ (say) that
(2)

they recognized their true love from the very first

time they met. We _____ (be)
(3)

all familiar with stories like these: A man

_____ (see) a woman across
(4)

a room, and he immediately _____ (recognize) his soul mate.[1] A woman
(5)

_____ (hear) a man's voice, and she _____ (feel) an instant
(6) (7)

attraction.

---

[1] **soul mate:** the perfect person for another person to marry

Some people may think, however, that these stories _____ (seem)
(8)
more like fantasy than real life. They believe that some couples _____ even
(9)
_____ (not like) each other at first, but then fall in love later.
(9)
In fact, some people _____ (think) that couples who fall in love quickly
(10)
are the same couples who end their relationships quickly. On the other hand, couples
who _____ (not have) an instant attraction take time to get to know each
(11)
other as friends. However, the best stories _____ (make) us believe in the
(12)
magic of love.

**2** Complete the review of a book about intuition.[1] Use the simple present form of the verbs in
the box. Sometimes more than one answer is possible. Use each verb only once.

| believe | give | live | say | travel |
|---------|------|------|-----|--------|
| ~~form~~ | have | not pay | teach | use |

We all _form_ first impressions when we use new products, go to new places, and meet
(1)
new people. We sometimes call these impressions or feelings "gut reactions," and our

intuition or instinct[2] causes them. Some people _____ that intuition is very
(2)
important and can help us live better lives. Shannon Healy is one such person.

Healy is a strong believer that all people have natural powers of intuition. In her book, she

_____ that most people, however, _____ enough attention
(3)                                                  (4)
to their "gut feelings."

Her new book, _Use Your Intuition_, is full of stories of people who _____
(5)
their intuition to find love and success. For example, a young woman makes a quick

decision between two job offers. She chooses one by paying attention to her "gut feeling"

that she will enjoy the work more, even though the pay is lower. It turns out to be a

good choice. Each chapter of Healy's book _____ a specific focus, such
(6)
as love, work, children, or health. The exercises in the book _____ people
(7)
practice on how to use their intuition to have success in all these areas.

---
[1]**intuition:** a quick sense of what is true or right | [2]**instinct:** a natural sense of what to do

Occasionally, Healy also _____ students about using the power of
(8)

intuition in workshops where she _____ – in Jacksonville, Florida. Some
(9)

people _____ hundreds of miles to attend her workshops. *Use Your Intuition*
(10)

is already a bestseller!

# Avoid Common Mistakes

**1** Circle the mistakes.

1. Even animals **seem** to form first impressions. I'm sure you have noticed they usually
   (a)
   (are reacting) quickly when they **meet** a new person.
   (b)                                (c)

2. **Do you think** instincts have anything to do with first impressions?
   (a)
   **Are we demonstrate** animal behavior when we **have** strong reactions to new people?
   (b)                                          (c)

3. Most people **don't make** strong impressions on me. Sometimes I **forget** their
   (a)                                                          (b)
   names almost immediately. However, I often **am having** strong reactions to different
   (c)
   geographic locations immediately.

4. Appearances **are** important the first time you **are meeting** someone. Everyone knows
   (a)                                      (b)
   that you **look** better if you are dressed nicely and if you smile.
   (c)

5. Right now, our new salesman **is making** a good first impression on everyone at the
   (a)
   meeting. He **is stand** straight, and he **is looking** at everyone there.
   (b)                          (c)

6. Some parents **are believing** that schools should **teach** children social skills.
   (a)                                            (b)
   They **feel** that making a good impression and working well in a group are very
   (c)
   important.

7. **I'm not have** a good time at this party. I **think** the food is bad and the music **is**
   (a)                                (b)                                          (c)
   too loud.

8. I **want** to look good at my sister's wedding, so I **try** to lose weight this month.
   (a)                                              (b)
   I **think** that I need to lose about eight pounds.
   (c)

**2** Find and correct eight more mistakes in the journal entry by a salesperson about making a good impression.

>     For salespeople, physical appearance is important, but there are other things that also
>                                                     *arrive*
> go into making a good first impression. For example, I always ~~am arriving~~ at meetings
> on time. I am knowing my clients are busy people, and I understand that their time is
> important. Also, I always call them by name. I even keep names and information about
> 5 clients in a special file online. In fact, I add information to that file this week.
>
>     In the past, I didn't pay much attention to body language. However, I am learn to be
> more conscious of the ways I move and how to use my hands effectively. At every meeting
> I am making eye contact – especially when I first greet a client and again when I leave.
> I practice my greetings in front of the mirror every day. I try to remember to smile. Of
> 10 course, I also want to look good. I have nice shoes, and I keep them clean and polished. I
> am thinking my new haircut makes me look good, too.
>
>     My sales numbers used to be a bit low, but they go up now. I am try to do better. I am
> knowing that I can be "Number One" in sales next year.

# Self-Assessment

Circle the word or phrase that correctly completes each sentence.

1. Some top salespeople _____ their greetings and handshakes before they meet their customers.

   a. are practicing    b. practice    c. practices

2. Jack _____ a lot of success as a salesman this year.

   a. is not having    b. has not    c. doesn't have

3. I need to get a suit for my job interview. A nice suit _____ about $300.00 at Guys' Clothing.

   a. costs    b. is costing    c. cost

4. Some people _____ in love the moment they first meet each other.

   a. falls    b. are falling    c. fall

5. I _____ enough money for a haircut even though I really need one.

   a. don't having    b. 'm not having    c. don't have

6.  Many animals depend on smell to form a first impression. They _____ as dependent on sight as people are.

    a. are        b. are not        c. are not being

7.  I _____ parties where I don't know anyone.

    a. don't like        b. 'm liking        c. 'm not liking

8.  _____ you _____ people's names immediately after you meet them?

    a. Do . . . using        b. Do . . . use        c. Are . . . use

9.  What behaviors _____ you _____ are the most damaging at a job interview?

    a. do . . . think        b. do . . . thinking        c. are . . . thinking

10. When Louisa takes a test, she decides which questions are the easiest. She answers those first, and then she answers the harder questions. Finally, she _____ all her answers one more time.

    a. reviews        b. is reviewing        c. review

11. A successful businessperson usually _____ on a positive attitude, hard work, and intuition.

    a. depends        b. depend        c. is depending

12. How do we _____ the success of a first meeting with someone else?

    a. measure        b. measures        c. measuring

13. The job fair _____ at 10:00 a.m.

    a. not open        b. opens        c. opening

14. This week, Bob _____ his salespeople a new way to make a better first impression.

    a. is teaching        b. teaching        c. teaches

15. Those salespeople _____ a very good first impression on the customers right now. Most of the customers are ignoring them as much as possible.

    a. don't make        b. aren't make        c. aren't making

# Simple Past and Past Progressive; *Used To, Would*

## Global Marketing

---

## Simple Past vs. Past Progressive

**1** Complete the article about one candy company's success. Use the simple past or past progressive form of the verbs in parentheses. Sometimes more than one answer is possible.

In 1982 *E.T.: The Extra-Terrestrial* <u>was</u> (be) a success for the movie company that
(1)

produced it – and it was also successful for a candy company. Here's what happened:

In the story, E.T. was an alien from outer space. He _____ (hide) in
(2)

the forest for a short time after his spaceship _____ (leave) Earth
(3)

without him. A young boy _____ (see) E.T. and decided to take him
(4)

home. The boy _____ (drop) pieces of candy on the ground all the
(5)

way to his house. He _____ (want) E.T. to follow the pieces of candy. It
(6)

worked. E.T. _____ (go) to the boy's house, and they became friends.
(7)

For a while, the movie company _____ (plan) to use a product
(8)

from another candy company. However, this company was not sure if it wanted its candy

in the film, and it _____ (take) some time to decide. When that candy
(9)

company _____ (say) no, another company _____
(10)                   (11)

(offer) its candy for the film. It was a newer product and not famous yet. As soon

as the movie came out, movie theaters were not only selling lots of tickets, they

_____ (sell) lots of the new candy, too. The sales of the new candy
(12)

went up dramatically.

**2** Complete the sentences about a garage sale.[1] Circle the correct form of the verbs.

1. My neighbors **got /(were getting)**ready to move to another city, so they(**decided**)/ **were deciding** to have a garage sale.

2. Because they were hoping to have a very successful sale, they **did / were doing** a little online research.

3. They soon **realized / were realizing** that effective advertising is a very important part of a successful sale.

4. They **placed / were placing** one small ad in the local newspaper and one online.

5. They **made / were making** signs and **placed / were placing** them around the neighborhood.

6. They **used / were using** "word of mouth" advertising[2] by telling all their friends and neighbors.

7. People **began / were beginning** to arrive at 6:30 a.m. for the sale. My neighbors **still got / were still getting** everything ready.

8. At 3:05 p.m. a car full of people **parked / was parking** in front of the house. Too late!

9. My neighbors **already counted / were already counting** their money from the sale and **put / were putting** unsold items in boxes to give to charity at that time.

10. The people were disappointed, but they **understood / were understanding** that they had come too late.

---

[1]**garage sale:** a sale of used household items (furniture, books, dishes, clothes) usually held in the front yard or garage of the house | [2]**"word of mouth" advertising:** an informal recommendation of a product between people

**3** Answer the questions. Use the simple past or past progressive. Write sentences that are true for you.

1. Did you ever sell anything when you were younger? What did you sell?

_____

2. Did you ever advertise anything when you were younger? How did you advertise it?

_____

3. What product made in another country did you buy this year?

_____

4. What were you looking for the last time you went shopping?

_____

5. Who were you shopping with the last time you went shopping?

_____

# Time Clauses with Simple Past and Past Progressive

**1** Each sentence describes two past events. Underline the words that describe the first event.

1. As soon as <u>Empire Clothing opened a store in Brazil</u>, they realized that they didn't understand the local culture very well.

2. Before they hired a Brazilian marketing expert to improve their image there, business was terrible.

3. Once the expert began talking with their marketing department, business began to improve.

4. Everyone relaxed a little when sales increased.

5. The marketing expert continued to work with the company until they learned how to adapt their advertising to the local culture.

**2** Complete the paragraph about an advertising experiment. Use the words in the box. Sometimes more than one answer is possible.

| after | as soon as | ~~before~~ | once | until | while |
|-------|-----------|-----------|------|-------|-------|

<u>*Before*</u> he did his famous experiment in 1957, James
<sub>(1)</sub>
Vicary was a little-known researcher who studied the

shopping habits of women. In his 1957 experiment, Vicary

said he flashed two different messages on the movie

screen _____ the film *Picnic* was playing.
<sub>(2)</sub>

Each message was on the screen for only a fraction of a

second, too short a time for anyone to actually "see" the message, and it appeared every

few seconds. One message said to drink a famous kind of soda, and the other one said

to eat popcorn. Vicary reported that sales of the famous soda went up 18.1 percent and

sales of popcorn went up 57.8 percent immediately _____ people watched
<sub>(3)</sub>

the film. _____ people heard about these amazing results, they became
<sub>(4)</sub>

worried about the power of what Vicary called subliminal[1] advertising. Vicary was

quite famous _____ other researchers repeated this study. They found *no*
<sub>(5)</sub>

increase in sales. _____ this information became public, Vicary admitted
<sub>(6)</sub>

that he had lied about the results of his experiment.

---

**subliminal:** below the level of what can be consciously seen

**3** Read each sentence. If it describes an action that interrupts an ongoing one, write *I* (for interrupting). If it describes two actions in progress at the same time, write *S* (for same).

1. When Matt was studying marketing at a university, he was also working in a part-time job at a marketing consultant company. __*S*__

2. He spontaneously decided to do a quick research study on consumer behavior at a local shopping mall while he was taking a class on market research. _____

3. While he was doing this research, he made an interesting discovery. _____

4. While he was interviewing people, he noticed that they blinked their eyes more quickly if they liked a product. _____

5. Later, when he was explaining his research results in a meeting at his company, his employers weren't paying attention. _____

6. When Matt was driving home, he was thinking about how uninterested they were. _____

7. While he was getting out of his car, he suddenly had an idea. _____

8. All during dinner, while he was eating, he was writing down his idea. _____

9. While Matt was in his last semester at school, he started a global marketing company and made a lot of money. _____

**4** Complete the sentences about people in the advertising and marketing departments at a company. Use the simple past or past progressive form of the verbs in parentheses.

1. While the people in the advertising department __*were discussing*__ (discuss) a new campaign, the marketing people __*had*__ (have) a brilliant idea.

2. When the boss _____ (hear) the marketing people's suggestion, he _____ (call) a meeting with the advertising team.

3. While the boss and the marketing team _____ (explain) their idea, the advertising people _____ (think) of ways to improve it.

4. The boss _____ (be) very pleased when he _____ (see) the two teams working together.

5. When the teams _____ (finish) the campaign, everyone _____ (need) a break.

6. So, as soon as the client _____ (approve) the campaign, the boss _____ (give) the two teams a week's vacation.

# Used To and Would

**1** Match the two parts of the sentences about how the marketing habits of a company have changed.

1. Until two years ago, my company __d__

2. The company didn't _____

3. They would _____

4. Last year, they hired a global director

    and _____

5. Now the company _____

a. use to have a global marketing director.

b. use the same ads in every country.

c. doesn't even use the same slogan in all
    markets.

~~d~~. used to spend very little on global marketing.

e. used different international campaigns.

That was a wise decision. Sales have been much better this year.

**2** Complete the sentences about advertising in the past. Use the simple past, *used to*, or *would* with the verbs in parentheses. Sometimes more than one answer is possible.

1. My grandfather never __used to want__ (want) to pay any money for advertising for his small business. One year, he even __put up__ (put up) homemade signs around town to save money.

2. In those days, though, he _____ (support) my baseball team every year.

3. Every year, granddad _____ (pay) for baseball shirts that had the name of his company on the front.

4. We _____ (wear) the shirts in every game.

5. One of my teammates _____ (not like) wearing his shirt, however. He hated it.

6. He always _____ (try) to wear another T-shirt instead.

7. Once, he even _____ (refuse) to wear any shirt at all!

8. That day, his father _____ (tell) him that my grandfather was helping him have a chance to play baseball.

9. After that he _____ (wear) the shirt in every game without complaining.

10. My grandfather _____ (do) a lot of advertising that way.

# Avoid Common Mistakes

**1** Circle the mistakes.

1. When business **was** good and the marketing company **was making** a lot of money, it
   (a)                                                                      (b)
   (used to giving) many parties for its employees.
   (c)

2. Carlos **was attending** a business meeting when he **realized** he did not have the chart
   (a)                                                    (b)
   he needed with him. He **asks** his secretary to get it for him.
   (c)

3. Christina **worked** for a small company in Boston when **she received** an offer to work
   (a)                                                              (b)
   for one of the largest marketing firms in the world. She **left** Boston to take the job.
   (c)

4. **Did you notice** all the product placements in the movie we just **see**? Many of them
   (a)                                                              (b)
   **seemed** especially inappropriate to me.
   (c)

5. Our product **was selling** well in some markets, and our company **planning** on
   (a)                                                          (b)
   introducing it to other markets as soon as it **was** possible.
   (c)

6. When Robert **was working** for an international company in Italy, he **meets** his wife.
   (a)                                                              (b)
   They **got married** in Rome.
   (c)

7. Omar and Hanan **were both studying** marketing while they **were raising** their two
   (a)                                                              (b)
   young children. Hanan's mother **used to helping** them a lot.
   (c)

8. Sylvia and Bob **worked** very hard for a big company when I first **met** them. Later they
   (a)                                                              (b)
   **decided** to leave and start a small business that focused on protecting the environment.
   (c)

**2** Find and correct eight more mistakes in this paragraph about a software design company.

> ABC Creative Software used to design software for the U.S. market only. They were
> doing very well and their business ‸*was* increasing every year. They would talking from time
> to time about "going global." Two years ago, the president of the company finally decides
> it was time to "go global." During the first year, they face many problems and global sales
> 5 are not good. Because they used to marketing their products to the United States only,
> they hired a consultant who helped them design better marketing strategies. Every week
> as the company developing, he would offer workshops in which he taught appropriate
> marketing strategies for different cultures. Soon sales were rising and the business doing
> very well. Soon after that, ABC Creative Software opened their first office in India. When
> 10 we called them recently, they celebrated this opening with a big party.

---

# Self-Assessment

Circle the word or phrase that correctly completes each sentence.

1. _____ they were introducing their new product in Japan, they were spending a great deal of money on advertising.

    a. While        b. Once        c. Until

2. While the employees _____ the new product, they were doing market research.

    a. developing        b. were developed        c. were developing

3. _____ the customers read the terrible safety record of the new airline, they stopped using it.

    a. Before        b. Until        c. Once

4. Cooper, Brennan, and Schmidt started advertising as soon as it _____ legal for lawyers to advertise.

    a. is        b. was        c. was being

5. Electronic Widgets _____ a new store in Phoenix, AZ, in 2011.

    a. opened        b. was opening        c. used to open

6. When the big car company in town went out of business, many people _____ for new jobs, because they were expecting the company to close soon.

    a. looked        b. were already looking        c. used to look

7. When Peter was growing up, he _____ part-time jobs in order to make money to help out his family.

    a. would often getting    b. would often get    c. used to getting

8. When customers stopped buying as many cars as they _____ buy, the company decided that it needed a new image.

    a. used to    b. were using to    c. use to

9. My husband's first book, *How to Market Anything*, was published in 2009. _____ it arrived in bookstores, he began to travel from city to city to advertise the book.

    a. Until    b. After    c. Before

10. When John worked in the marketing department of Allied Software, he never _____ a day of work.

    a. was missing    b. misses    c. missed

11. While Marcia was discussing recent sales with her sales team, her supervisor called her and _____ her to come to her office immediately.

    a. would tell    b. told    c. was telling

12. _____ Emin could leave Istanbul for a business meeting in New York, he had to get a visa.

    a. After    b. Before    c. Until

13. That actor made a lot of money selling products on TV _____ he did something that made people dislike him.

    a. while    b. as soon as    c. until

14. That company _____ one of the most famous commercials of all time in 1997.

    a. created    b. was creating    c. used to create

15. Our company _____ pay much attention to our customers in South America, and we lost a lot of their business.

    a. didn't use to    b. used to    c. would

# UNIT 3

## Present Perfect and Present Perfect Progressive

### Success

## Present Perfect

**1** Read the paragraph about Eric and his wife, Michelle. Then label the bold and underlined verbs *U* (unspecified time in the past), *C* (time that continues to the present), or *R* (recent action) according to the use of the present perfect.

    Eric **has just received** a really good job offer to manage a store in another town,
           (1)
Springfield. When Eric tells his wife, Michelle, about the job offer, she is pleased and

says, "Oh, that's wonderful. **I've wanted** to live in Springfield for so long." Eric says,
                                  (2)
"Great. **I've been** worried about telling you all day. My boss **has discovered** that the
      (3)                                      (4)
Springfield store isn't making much money, and he wants me to help change that.

He **has just offered** me a raise with the new job." "Well," Michelle says, "it's a great
    (5)
opportunity. So far we **have been able to** save some money for the children's college
               (6)
education, but we'll certainly need more." Michelle agrees that the job would be a good

move, and Eric decides to take the job.

**2** Unscramble the sentences about Henry Chen's political career. Use the present perfect form of the verbs. Sometimes more than one answer is possible.

1. all his life / Henry Chen / an elected official / want / to be

   *Henry Chen has wanted to be an elected official all his life.*

2. for / he / live / 15 years / in Cupertino, California

   _____

3. he / for city council[1] four times / run / in the last several years

   _____

4. so far / not win / he / any election in his town

   _____

5. just / he / decide / to run for the school board[2]

   _____

[1]**city council:** a group of elected people who make or change the laws of a city | [2]**school board:** a group of people who make decisions about how to manage a school

**18**

6. not give up / Henry / still / on his dream

_____

7. never / he / become / discouraged

_____

**3** Complete the sentences about a movie with _since_ or _for_.

_Our Success_ is a real success at the box office!

1. The movie has made $80 million _<u>since</u>_ it opened.

2. It has been the most-watched movie _____ two months.

3. Attendance has gone up every week _____ the last three months.

4. Jason Prince, one of the stars, has not had a hit movie _____ several years.

5. Laura Noble, the other star, has been an actress _____ she was a teenager.

6. People have seen the two stars out together in public _____ the movie appeared in theaters.

# Present Perfect vs. Simple Past

**1** Complete the conversation. Use the present perfect or simple past form of the verbs in parentheses. Use contractions when possible.

**Tarek:** _<u>Have</u>_ you _<u>talked</u>_ (talk) to Michael lately? What's he doing these days?
(1)     (1)

**Daisuke:** I'm not sure. I know he _____ (finish) college two years ago, but I
(2)

_____ (not hear) anything about him since then.
(3)

**Tarek:** What about Peng?

**Daisuke:** Oh, he _____ (move) to San José. He _____ (get) a
(4)     (5)

new job a few months ago.

**Tarek:** _____ his kids _____ (start) school yet?
(6)     (6)

**Daisuke:** I'm not sure. I _____ (not keep) in close touch with Peng
(7)

for a while. I know that he _____ (be) very successful in
(8)

his work, though.

**2** Complete the paragraphs about a convict who escaped from prison. Use the present perfect or simple past form of the verbs in the box.

| arrest | buy | give | receive | see |
|--------|-----|------|---------|-----|
| ~~be~~ | escape | not have | say | stop |

Robert "Hoodie" Hudson <u>has been</u> on the FBI's Most Wanted List
                                    (1)

since he _____ from a prison in Texas 10 years ago. People
                    (2)

_____ him in several states since that time. FBI agents
            (3)

_____ never _____ their search for him over the years,
      (4)                      (4)

but up until now they _____ any success.
                                (5)

Last week, however, the FBI _____ a call from a woman
                                          (6)

who _____ she was Hudson's former girlfriend. She said,
              (7)

"Hoodie _____ just _____ a plane ticket for Paris." She
            (8)                  (8)

_____ them his address in Austin, Texas. The FBI called the police in
          (9)

Austin, who _____ Hudson the same day. Hudson is now back in prison.
                      (10)

Another success for law enforcement!

**MOST WANTED**

**ROBERT "HOODIE" HUDSON**

---

# Present Perfect vs. Present Perfect Progressive

**1** Write questions about famous people. Then answer the questions with the words in parentheses and *since* or *for*. Use the present perfect progressive.

1. How long / Bill and Melinda Gates / run / their foundation

**Q:** <u>*How long have Bill and Melinda Gates been running their foundation?*</u>

**A:** <u>*They have been running it for about 20 years.*</u> (about 20 years)

2. How long / Oprah Winfrey / work / in TV?

**Q:** _____

**A:** _____
   (the 1970s)

3. How long / Venus and Serena Williams / play / tennis?

**Q:** _____

**A:** _____
   (more than 20 years)

4. How long / Neil deGrasse Tyson / host / the TV show *NOVA scienceNOW*?

Q:_____

A:_____

   (2006)

5. How long / Lang Lang / play / the piano?

Q:_____

A:_____

   (he was three years old)

**2** Complete the article about Emily's college preparations. Circle the correct verb forms. Sometimes more than one answer is possible.

### Preparing for Success

Emily is a junior at the local high school. She

~~has planned / has been planning~~ to go to college all her
   (1)

life. She **hasn't decided / hasn't been deciding** yet whether
   (2)

she wants to be a social worker or a medical researcher, but

she knows she wants to contribute something to the world

through her work.

Emily and her parents **have visited / have been visiting**
   (3)

colleges lately. They **have seen / have been seeing** five schools so far, and they plan
   (4)

to visit three more. Emily **has spent / has been spending** a lot of time recently on
   (5)

her college applications. She **has written / has been writing** all of her essays for the
   (6)

applications already. She **has asked / has been asking** several people to read the essays
   (7)

for her. They **have all made / have all been making** suggestions, so Emily is now
   (8)

rewriting her essays to improve them.

"All of us **have worked / have been working** day and night for several months on
   (9)

getting Emily into a good school," say her parents. Her two older brothers and a sister

**have graduated / have been graduating** from college already, and now they have good
   (10)

jobs. They **have had / have been having** a hard time realizing that their "baby sister" is
   (11)

almost ready to go to college.

**3** Complete the paragraphs about successful people. Use the present perfect or present perfect progressive form of the verbs in parentheses. Use each form at least once in each paragraph. Sometimes more than one answer is possible.

Michael _has been inventing_ (invent) things since he was a child. This year he
_____ (already / invent) three new household gadgets.
(2)

When Mohamed arrived in London in 1995, he was already 34 years old.

Success _____ (not come) easily to him.
(3)

He _____ (have) to work very hard. Since 2005, though,
(4)

he _____ (run) one of the most successful employment
(5)

agencies in London.

Sarah _____ (be) a very successful hairdresser for years.
(6)

She decided to become a hairdresser when she was in middle school. Recently, she

_____ (think) about opening her own salon.
(7)

**4** Complete each person's statement with the present perfect or present perfect progressive form of the verbs in parentheses. Use each form at least once in each statement. Sometimes more than one answer is possible.

**Helen:** I _have had_ (have) two husbands. My first husband died in 1999 after our children
(1)

were grown. My second husband and I _____ (be)
(2)

married since 2003. He and I _____ (live) in Oakmont
(3)

Village for nine years. I _____ (love) both my husbands,
(4)

and I'm proud of my children. My life has been a big success!

**Tomás:** I was an accountant for a global corporation for many years. I retired in 2007 and

moved to Oakmont Village. I _____ (do) volunteer work
(5)

at the hospital every week since then. I _____ also _____ (take)
(6)                          (6)

a lot of courses at the local community college over the years – Spanish,

nineteenth-century history, and even yoga. I think I've had a great life!

**Isabel:** I don't live in Oakmont Village. I'm here visiting my Brazilian friend

Raquel, who _____ (live) here since 2006. I
(7)

_____ (come) to see her here every summer since 2007.
(8)

Raquel _____ (live) in several countries before this and
(9)

_____ (have) several careers. She's a really interesting
(10)

person.

# Avoid Common Mistakes

**1** Circle the mistakes.

1. Jordan (is living) in Rome since 2010. Her business **has been** very successful there, and
   (a)        (b)
   she **has been making** a lot of money lately.
   (c)

2. The news report about the winning design **have been** on TV every hour. They
   (a)
   **have already interviewed** everybody in the company, but they **haven't talked** to the
   (b)        (c)
   designers yet.

3. Daniel's parents **have bought** him a nice used car. He **has promised** to be a responsible
   (a)        (b)
   driver, and he **has driving** carefully so far.
   (c)

4. Since her daughter was born last year, my sister **is changing** her ideas about success.
   (a)
   She **hasn't given up** her career or anything like that, but she **has been giving** much
   (b)        (c)
   more attention to her family and her personal life lately.

5. Greg **has been selling** three cars this week. He **has made** $4,000 in commissions since
   (a)        (b)
   Monday, and his boss **has been talking** about a possible promotion.
   (c)

6. For several years, Theresa **has been growing** wonderful roses, which she **has selling** to
   (a)        (b)
   a local flower shop. Now, she **has decided** to retire and let her children run the business.
   (c)

7. Matthew and Amanda **are practicing** their Spanish every day for the past month.
   (a)
   Amanda's company **has opened** a new office in Spain, and her boss **has offered** her the
   (b)        (c)
   management position there.

8. **Have you been hearing** that the Swift Aircraft Company won a fifty-million-dollar
   (a)
   contract from that Chinese airline? They **have been trying** to get that contract for two
   (b)
   years! Now, they **have been celebrating** it for two days.
   (c)

**2** Find and correct eight more mistakes in the paragraphs about a businessman's retirement.

Tom Wilson retired last year after a long, successful career in business. Since he

retired, he has remodeled[1] the kitchen and has ~~been painting~~ *painted* the whole house. Now that

it is finished, it looks new again! Tom and his wife, Barbara, has also taken a few golf

lessons and have golfing once a week at the local golf course. Tom has a lot of extra time

5 and energy and have begun to do some of the cooking and cleaning. Barbara has had her

own ways of doing things for years, and she has trying to find a nice way to tell Tom that

he needs to find something else to keep him busy.

Fortunately, the other day Tom ran into another retired businessman from his

company who told him that he is doing volunteer work since last year at the Local

10 Business Association (LBA). He said he has been very happy and busy ever since he

started. He told Tom that for the last few months he is helping a Vietnamese couple with

their new business. Tom has already been calling the LBA twice today to volunteer, too.

He has been having to leave a message both times, but when they call him back, he'll set

up a day to begin. Now his retirement will be a real success!

---

[1] **remodel:** change to make better

# Self-Assessment

Circle the word or phrase that correctly completes each sentence.

1. Manuel Chapple _____ great films for years, but he has never won an Academy Award.

   a. has made    b. made    c. makes

2. I've _____ that there is going to be a new film about the recent election this year.

   a. hear    b. heard    c. hearing

3. Kyle Desch _____ a successful campaign for governor a few years ago.

   a. ran    b. has run    c. have run

4. Soraya Samanta _____ about running for Congress recently.

   a. is thinking    b. has thinking    c. has been thinking

5.  When she was 28 years old, Verónica _____ a successful career in the office of a university foundation to become a nurse.

    a. left     b. has left     c. leaves

6.  How long _____ a manager now?

    a. is Paul being     b. has Paul being     c. has Paul been

7.  Books about how to become a successful person _____ never _____ more popular.

    a. have . . . been     b. has . . . be     c. has . . . been

8.  *Think Yourself to Success* has been _____ thousands of copies a year for 10 years.

    a. sold     b. selling     c. sell

9.  Has your cousin started her organization to defend ethnic minorities' rights _____ ? She used to say this was one of her main goals in life when we were in college.

    a. yet     b. since     c. ever

10. My uncle's store was very successful for a while, but recently sales _____ down.

    a. have been going     b. has gone     c. go

11. My father _____ to play tennis when he was 40. He's 60 now, and he still plays.

    a. learns     b. learned     c. has been learning

12. My friend Brian had two hit TV shows in the 1990s, but he has not had another hit show _____ several years.

    a. yet     b. in     c. since

13. My parents have been married for 50 years. They _____ their Golden Wedding Anniversary yesterday.

    a. have celebrated     b. have been celebrating     c. celebrated

14. The owner of our company is very happy that most of her employees _____ with the company for many years.

    a. are     b. has been     c. have been

15. Only three people _____ our department since 2011, and two of those people retired.

    a. leave     b. has left     c. have left

# Past Perfect
# and Past Perfect Progressive

## Nature vs. Nurture

---

## Past Perfect

**1** Complete the conversation about a novel by the American author Mark Twain (1835–1910). Use the past perfect form of the verbs in parentheses. Use contractions when possible.

**A:** Have you ever read *Pudd'nhead Wilson*, by Mark Twain?

It's a novel that says that environment is more important

than genetics.

**B:** No, I haven't read it. What's it about?

**A:** Well, the United States <u>*had abolished*</u> (abolish)
(1)

slavery by 1894, when Twain wrote the novel, but people

_____ (not forget) slavery or the
(2)

Civil War, which ended slavery.

**B:** Is it about slavery, then? Tell me about the story.

**A:** Well, it starts in 1830s Missouri. A beautiful young slave, who was named Roxy,

_____ (just / give) birth to a boy. The slave owner, Percy
(3)

Driscoll, had an infant son, Tom, who _____ (be born) on the
(4)

same day. The two babies looked similar. Because Roxy was only 1/16 African, she and her

son both looked white.

**B:** Is that important?

**A:** Yes. Roxy _____ (become) worried that Driscoll was going to
(5)

sell her infant son, Chambers, to a slave owner in another state. She wanted to keep her

son near, so because the two babies looked alike, she decided to switch them. Her boy,

Chambers, became "Tom" and lived with the slave owner's family as their son. The slave

owner's son, Tom, became her son, "Chambers," and grew up as a slave. Because she

_____ (make) the switch, Roxy was able to watch her real son
(6)

grow up near her.

**B:** This is starting to get confusing. I guess I need to remember that "Tom" was really

Chambers, and "Chambers" was really Tom. Right?

**A:** Right. Anyway, by 1850 or so, because of the switch that Roxy had made, "Tom"

_____ (grow up) as the son of a rich landowner and
(7)

_____ (become) a cruel, selfish person. Finally, he killed
(8)

someone. When they investigated the murder, everybody learned that "Tom"

_____ (commit) the crime. They also learned that Roxy
(9)

_____ (switch) the two boys.
(10)

**B:** What happened to "Chambers," the real Tom, who was the real son of the slave owner?

**A:** After they discovered the switch, he was freed. Unfortunately, he still felt like a slave,

though. He _____ (never / learn) to read and write, and he
(11)

talked like a slave, so he wasn't comfortable as a free, rich, white man.

**2** Complete the sentences about Carol, a mother of twins, and her experience enrolling them
in school. Use the past perfect.

1. Carol / already have / several meetings with the principal.

    Before their first day of school, _Carol had already had several meetings with the principal_ .

2. the mother / ask / to keep the twins together

    _____ , but the school put them in different classes.

3. they / always do / everything together

    That first day of school, the twins were very scared because _____ .

4. the twins / not make / any friends in class

    By the first week of school, the teachers noticed that _____ .

5. the twins / be / sick / for four days

    By the second week of school, _____ .

6. they / always get along / well

    Carol also noticed that the twins fought more. Before, _____ .

7. the twins' teachers / go / to the principal with their concerns

    Carol didn't know it, but _____ .

8. the teachers / put / them in the same class

    A few days later, when the twins arrived at school, _____ .

# Past Perfect with Time Clauses

**1** Complete the story about Dolly the sheep. Use *after*, *as soon as*, *before*, *by the time*, *until*, or *when*. Use each word at least once. Sometimes more than one answer is possible.

Many people had never even heard the word "clone"[1] <u>until</u>
(1)
they read about a sheep named Dolly. _____
(2)
newspapers around the world carried the story of how

scientists had successfully cloned Dolly, it seemed everybody

was talking about cloning. People talked about cloning as if

it were something completely new that had never happened

before. Actually, _____ scientists cloned Dolly,
(3)
there had already been a lot of small cloning successes in research laboratories. What

made Dolly different was that scientists had cloned her from an *adult* sheep cell, not an

embryonic[2] one.

_____ people learned about Dolly's cloning, they thought the idea was
(4)
very controversial. A debate began about whether cloning is a good thing to do or not.

_____ Dolly was born, most people had only heard about someone creating
(5)
life in a laboratory in books like *Frankenstein*, by Mary Shelley. _____ Dolly was
(6)
born, however, people had to think very hard about what cloning might mean in the future.

_____ Dolly died in 2003, she had only lived for six years, but
(7)
_____ she died, she had been a completely normal sheep, except for
(8)
having no father!

---

[1]**clone:** an exact genetic copy of a plant or animal created from a single cell | [2]**embryonic:** from an unborn baby

**2** Write sentences about the twins Mariel and Marcie and their imaginary friend,[1] "Chippy." Use the past perfect and simple past.

1. when / Mariel and Marcie / be / ready to start school / they / already / have / an imaginary friend for two years

   *When Mariel and Marcie were ready to start school, they had already*
   *had an imaginary friend for two years.*

2. before / school / start / they / play / with Chippy all summer

   _____

   _____

---

[1]**imaginary friend:** an unreal person that some children create in their imagination and treat like a real person and friend

3. after / their parents / do / research on imaginary friends / they / decide / to talk to a psychologist

_____

4. before / their parents / make / an appointment with the psychologist / they / read a lot about the topic

_____

5. when / they / talk / to the psychologist / he / already / spend / 30 minutes with the twins

_____

6. by the time / they / leave / the psychologist's office / their parents / learn / that the twins were normal

_____

# Past Perfect Progressive

**1** Complete the sentences about a family with the past perfect progressive form of the verbs in parentheses. Use contractions when possible.

When Angela got home from shopping, . . .

1. Her sons Doug and Jason _had been watching_ (watch) TV for a couple of hours.

2. Her daughter, Alison, _____ (talk) on her cell phone for hours.

3. None of them _____ (work) on their homework.

4. The water outside _____ (run) since she left the house.

5. Her son Peter _____ (play) in the water and was completely covered with water and mud.

6. Her husband, Mark, _____ (pay) bills online.

7. The whole family _____ (not pay) attention to Brutus, the puppy.

8. Brutus _____ (chew) on a pair of expensive sneakers the whole time.

**2** Complete the sentences about Oprah Winfrey's life and work. Circle the correct verbs. Sometimes more than one answer is possible.

1. Oprah Winfrey (had been living) / **lived** with her grandmother for the first six years of her life when her mother took her to live in Milwaukee.

2. After her mother **had been having** / **had had** difficulty with Oprah as a teenager, she sent her to live with her father in Tennessee.

3. Oprah became an honors student and an excellent public speaker after she **had been paying** / **had paid** more attention to her schoolwork for a while.

4. Oprah earned a full scholarship to attend Tennessee State University in Nashville after she **had been winning** / **had won** an oratory contest.

5. As an adult, in Chicago, Oprah **had been working** / **had worked** at a TV station for less than three years when they changed the name of her show to *The Oprah Winfrey Show* and they broadcast it nationally.

6. She had also co-starred in a miniseries while she **had been hosting** / **had hosted** *The Oprah Winfrey Show*.

7. After she **had been doing** / **had done** her TV show for about ten years, she decided to start Oprah's Book Club.

8. She **had been sharing** / **had shared** information about her own life with her fans for years before she found out in 2010 that she had a half-sister.

9. She **had been planning** / **had planned** to start her own TV network in 2009, but it didn't actually begin until January of 2011.

10. She **had been interviewing** / **had interviewed** people on television for over 30 years when she finally ended *The Oprah Winfrey Show*.

11. When *The Oprah Winfrey Show* ended, Oprah **had been appearing** / **had appeared** nine times on *Time* magazine's list of most influential people.

# Avoid Common Mistakes

**1** Circle the mistakes.

1. John's twin brother **went** to prison for the first time a couple of years ago. This wasn't a
   (a)
   surprise because he (got) into trouble with the police ever since he **was** a teenager.
   (b)                                                                    (c)

2. Krish was about two inches taller than his twin brother, Rajat. The doctors thought that
   this **was** because Rajat **has had** a severe illness when he **was** 10 years old.
   (a)                      (b)                            (c)

3. My twin sisters, Jennifer and Jessica, **have visited** several colleges before they **decided**
   (a)                                                                                    (b)
   to apply to Washington State. They **considered** a lot of things, such as distance
   (c)
   and cost.

4. Before Diego and Ariel **got** married, they **have decided** to move to Ariel's hometown,
   <sub>(a)</sub>                                       <sub>(b)</sub>
   so they would be closer to her family. By the time they moved, Ariel **hadn't lived** in her
                                                                   <sub>(c)</sub>
   town for over a decade.

5. The twins Mark and Matt **had been graduating** from high school before their family
                                            <sub>(a)</sub>
   **moved** to California. Mark went with their parents, but Matt **chose** to go to a school on
   <sub>(b)</sub>                                                    <sub>(c)</sub>
   the East Coast.

6. Before Dr. Wilson **began** his research, he **hadn't realized** that several other scientists
                                       <sub>(a)</sub>                     <sub>(b)</sub>
   **have already been studying** the "nature vs. nurture" issue.
                    <sub>(c)</sub>

7. Many years ago, I **saw** someone in the supermarket who I **haven't seen** in a couple of
                      <sub>(a)</sub>                                       <sub>(b)</sub>
   months. When I called, "Yawen," and said hello, she told me she **wasn't** Yawen. She was
                                                                            <sub>(c)</sub>
   Yawen's twin sister, Ying.

8. The police said that they **had arrested** Nick because he **had attacked** a co-worker at
                                    <sub>(a)</sub>                            <sub>(b)</sub>
   lunch. He explained that it was because he **had** a bad day.
                                                <sub>(c)</sub>

**2** Find and correct eight more mistakes in the paragraph about searching for a twin.

>     When Mary's daughter was 10 years old, Mary told her a story about when she ~~has~~ *had*
>
> been a young girl herself. She said that until she was about 10 years old, she has always
>
> believed that she had a twin sister somewhere. Her parents had laughed and had said
>
> that that was because she read too many stories about twins. Mary told her daughter
>
> 5 that one day, she has discovered a box of photos on the top shelf in a cupboard. She said
>
> it looked as if it has been there a long time. The box contained an old photo of two little
>
> girls who appeared to be about two years old. Mary said she immediately thought that
>
> the photo was a picture of her and her missing "twin sister." She took it to her mother,
>
> who began to cry. She told Mary that someone had been taking the photo of herself and
>
> 10 her twin sister 40 years before, but then a short time later, her sister had been dying in an
>
> accident. All along Mary has thought there was a "missing twin," but now she knew it had
>
> been being her mother's twin, not hers.

# Self-Assessment

Circle the word or phrase that correctly completes each sentence.

1. My sister was shocked when she found out she was going to have twins. No one in our family _____ twins before.

   a. had been having     b. had had     c. had

2. In 2011, Mona tried to find her adoption records, but the adoption agency _____ .

   a. had already closed     b. has already been closing     c. has already closed

3. Scientists around the world _____ "nature versus nurture" for several years when they released their results.

   a. studied     b. has been studying     c. had been studying

4. Felicia's parents _____ her adoption papers since her birth, so she did not know she was adopted.

   a. hid     b. had hidden     c. have hidden

5. Seth and Eric _____ participants in several studies about twins before they began college.

   a. had been     b. had been being     c. have been

6. Until Matthew's parents both _____ , he hadn't known that he was adopted. He found his adoption papers in the attic of the house they left for him.

   a. died     b. have died     c. had been dying

7. The college did not hire Dr. Peters because he _____ had enough experience teaching.

   a. did not     b. have not     c. had not

8. When Joe finally paid off his student loans for his teaching degree, he _____ for ten years.

   a. had been teaching     b. has been teaching     c. is teaching

9. _____ Beth had learned that she had a twin sister, she spent years looking for her.

   a. Before     b. By the time     c. After

10. How many twins _____ Dr. Chang _____ before she published her article in *Genetics Today*?

    a. had . . . studied     b. has . . . studied     c. had . . . studying

11. Neither Julia nor her brother Jason had known they were adopted until one of their cousins _____ them when they were teenagers.

    a. had been telling     b. told     c. has told

12. Several years _____ by the time the scientists decided to start their experiments again.

    a. had passed     b. have passed     c. had been passing

13. The courthouse _____ by the time Brianna tried to research her family history, so she was not able to find the records she needed.

    a. had burned down     b. had burn down     c. has burned down

14. The research assistant had _____ played an important role in the twins study when Dr. Clark decided to add her name to the study as an author.

    a. before     b. as soon as     c. already

15. Paul _____ about opening a store just for twins until his wife told him that she thought it was a bad idea.

    a. had thinking     b. has been thinking     c. had been thinking

# Be Going To, Present Progressive, and Future Progressive

## Looking Ahead at Technology

# Be Going To, Present Progressive, and Simple Present for Future

**1** Circle the best form of each verb to complete the conversation. Remember that the present progressive is used to express definite plans or arrangements and *be going to* is used to express general intentions and plans for the future.

**John:** Su Ho! I didn't know you were in town!

How's life in Hong Kong?

**Su Ho:** Hey, John! Life has been great over there. I'm here in New York for business meetings for a couple of weeks. I was going to call you.

**John:** Oh, will you be here next week?

**I'm going to get / (I'm getting)** married next
(1)
Saturday. Can you come to the wedding? **We're holding / We're going to hold** the
(2)
ceremony right here in the neighborhood. Do you think you can make it?

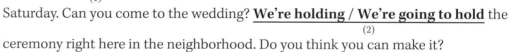

**Su Ho:** I'm not sure **I'm going to have / I'm having** time. **We're going to have / We're having**
(3)                                    (4)
several meetings next week in L.A., and we might have one on Saturday.

**John:** Please try to come. Marina's family **is flying / is going to fly** here tomorrow
(5)
morning. **They're all staying / They're all going to stay** at the Flamingo Hotel. We
(6)
could probably make a reservation for you there, too.

**Su Ho:** That would be great. I think **I'm probably going to come / I'm probably coming**.
(7)
I'll call you as soon as I know. I just have to check with my boss.

**John:** OK. **I'm going to make sure / I'm making sure** there's a place for you at the
(8)
hotel. Anyway, if you can't come, you can still watch the wedding. A friend of ours

**is setting up / is going to set up** a video feed[1] just before the ceremony, so you'll be
  (9)

able to watch it on your laptop from wherever you are. Isn't technology great?

___

[1]**video feed:** a video of an event shown live on the Internet

**2** Complete Fatih's e-mail to her friend Sanjay. Use *be going to*, the present progressive, or the simple present with the verbs in parentheses. Remember to use the simple present for scheduled events or timetables. Sometimes more than one answer is possible.

Hi, Sanjay,

I think you will finally have the opportunity to meet my boss, Dr. Simmons.

Dr. Simmons *is leaving* (leave) for Chicago tomorrow for the conference.
          (1)

Everything is arranged. I _____ (take) him to the
                      (2)

airport at noon, and then I _____ (teach) his class
                        (3)

for him on Tuesday morning. You will be able to talk to Dr. Simmons at the

conference. The conference _____ (open) on Tuesday
                      (4)

at 10:00 a.m. Dr. Ramesh Gupta _____ (give) the
                        (5)

opening address,[1] and Dr. Simmons _____ (speak) in
                          (6)

the afternoon. There _____ (be) a "meet-and-greet"
                (7)

party from 5:00–6:00, and then dinner _____ (start)
                          (8)

at 6:30. Dr. Simmons _____ (attend) the party, but I'm
                (9)

not sure if he _____ (go) to the dinner. If you would like
          (10)

to talk with him about your research, the meet-and-greet party is probably your

best opportunity. He _____ (fly) home the following
                (11)

morning at 8:00 a.m.

Good luck,

Fatih

___

[1]**opening address:** the first speech at a conference, meeting, etc.

**3** Write four sentences about things you plan or intend to do, or things that you don't plan or intend to do. Use *be going to* or the present progressive. Use *not* when necessary. Write sentences that are true for you.

1. _____

2. _____

3. _____

4. _____

## *Will* and *Be Going To*

**1** Complete the predictions in the blog with the correct form of the verbs in parentheses. Use *be going to* when there is present evidence for the prediction and *will* when there is no evidence.

---

### How will technology change in the future?
#### What do you think?

**Kate09:** Small handheld computers and smartphones are becoming really popular. People *aren't going to use* (not use) desktop computers
(1)
at all in the future.

**JackH:** I really don't know. Maybe smartphones

_____ (get) smaller.
(2)

**SMI960:** Every year companies make products that are easier to use. In the future, technology _____ (be) even
(3)
easier to use.

**EvenTech:** I really think that someone _____ (invent)
(4)
a way to send messages without typing or even speaking. It would be great if you could just think of a message, and your phone would send it.

**ShellyB:** People might wear smart clothing in the future, but in my opinion, this _____ (not happen) anytime soon.
(5)

**DrJHP:** Right now a lot of doctors are using computers for patient information. They even use computers in the exam room during appointments. In the future, people _____ (not fill out)
(6)
forms on paper in doctors' offices.

---

**2** Complete the conversations between different members of a family. Use *be going to* for predictions based on present evidence and *will* for requests, offers, promises, and decisions made at the time of speaking. Use contractions when possible.

**A Husband:** The remote control for the TV doesn't work. It

needs new batteries.

   **Wife:** Hmm, I don't think we have any batteries at home.

**Husband:** I _'ll go_ (go) to the store and get some.
           (1)

   **Wife:** That's not necessary. I don't think that

   I _____ (watch) any TV this evening. I feel like going out.
           (2)

**B   Mother:** Where's your homework? I _____ (check) it now if you'd like.
                                      (3)

     **Son:** I haven't finished it yet.

  **Mother:** If you finish your homework early, I promise I _____ (let) you
                                                          (4)

  watch a movie on our new 3D TV.

**C   Sister:** _____ you please _____ (turn down) the music? I'm trying
              (5)                    (5)
  to study!

  **Brother:** Hmm. I _____ (do) that if you let me borrow your smartphone.
                    (6)

**3** Write predictions about the future with information that is true for you. Write sentences with *will*. Then use *be going to* to write sentences that give evidence for the prediction.

   *Will*

   1. _____

   2. _____

   3. _____

   *Be Going To*

   4. _____

   5. _____

   6. _____

# Future Progressive

**1** Complete the story about a woman who is going to another country for an operation. Use the verbs in the box and the future progressive with *will* or *be going to*. Sometimes more than one answer is possible.

| give | pick | recover | spend | stay | take | ~~travel~~ | wait |

## Medical Tourism[1] Is Growing

Helen Browning *will be traveling* OR *is going to be traveling* to Bangalore, India,
(1)
next week to have a heart operation. A car _____ her up
(2)
at the airport in Mumbai. It's going to take her directly to the hotel, where she

_____ the night. The next day she will fly from Mumbai to
(3)
Bangalore. A driver _____ for her there to take her to the
(4)
hospital. She _____ in the hospital that night.
(5)

In the morning, Helen has an appointment with Dr. Kothari, a specialist in heart surgery.

He _____ her a number of tests throughout the morning.
(6)
Her operation is scheduled for 9:00 a.m. the following day. After the operation, she

_____ in the hospital for about five days before they let her
(7)
go home. The excellent nursing staff at the hospital _____
(8)
very good care of her during all this time.

[1]**medical tourism:** the act of traveling to another location for health care, usually at a less expensive cost than in one's home country

**2** Complete the conversations about future plans. Use the verbs in parentheses. Conversation A is less formal (between sisters) and conversation B is more formal (a newspaper interview). Use the future progressive with *will* or *be going to*, depending on what is appropriate for each conversation.

**A Mary's sister:** What *are* you and John *going to do* (do) this summer?
(1)          (1)

**Mary Lawson:** John _____ (travel) for the next two months advertising
(2)
his new book, *The Future Is Coming*. He _____ (talk)
(3)
about his book on TV and in bookstores.

**Mary's sister:** _____ you _____ (travel) with him?
(4)          (4)

**Mary Lawson:** No, I _____ (work) on my own book, *The Future Is*
(5)
*Already Here.*

**B** **Reporter:** What _____ you and Dr. Lawson _____ (do)
                                    (6)                                                          (6)
this summer?

**Mary Lawson:** Dr. Lawson _____ (travel) for the next two
                                                  (7)
months advertising his new book, *The Future is Coming.*

He _____ (talk) about his book on TV and
                    (8)
in bookstores.

**Reporter:** _____ you _____ (travel) with him?
                          (9)                                (9)

**Mary Lawson:** No, I _____ (work) on my own book, *The Future Is*
                                      (10)
*Already Here.*

# Avoid Common Mistakes

**1** Circle the mistakes.

1. I **told** everyone in the office not to text me for any reason on Saturday. I (**will attend**) my
      (a)                                                                                                                        (b)
sister's graduation in San Diego. I **will be** back in the office on Monday.
                                                              (c)

2. Look at your train schedule. I think the train to Phoenix **leaves** at 1:00 or 2:00 p.m.
                                                                                          (a)
I don't think any trains **will be leaving** earlier. I **going to wait** for you in the Phoenix
                                          (b)                              (c)
station café.

3. When **do you think** the engineers **going to realize** that they **need** to improve the
                  (a)                                    (b)                          (c)
latest tablet?

4. My company says in the company newsletter that it **will install** a totally wireless
                                                                                  (a)
communication system during the summer next year. I **think** that **will be** a good thing.
                                                                                  (b)                    (c)

5. TopStar Communications **is closing** early one day next week. The IT department
                                            (a)
**going to do** work all night, so you **will not be able** to access your accounts during that time.
      (b)                                              (c)

6. According to the schedule, the afternoon talks on new electronic devices **will begin**
                                                                                                              (a)
at 2:00. We**'re not going to arrive** until 3:00. The presenters **will discuss** new devices
                  (b)                                                            (c)
when we get there.

7. *Technology World* **is predicting** that by 2020 all of us **are going to be driving** electric
                                (a)                                                      (b)
cars. I **going to wait** until 2020 before I buy a new car.
            (c)

8. The workmen **will move** new workstations into the office for the next few hours.
                        (a)
Everyone **is going** home at lunch and **won't come back** until tomorrow.
                  (b)                                            (c)

**2** Find and correct the mistakes in the memo from a manager at a clothing business.

>       The April issue of the magazine *Future Trends* says that in the year 2030, people will
>
> ~~wear~~ *be wearing* disposable clothing every day. If this prediction is correct, it going to have a big
>
> impact on our clothing business. We going to need to begin researching and developing
>
> ideas for creating clothing that people can wear once and then throw away.
>
> 5      Discussion of this topic starts tomorrow at our weekly idea meeting in Conference
>
> Room A. I'll travel next week in South Carolina to see our factories, and I am going to be
>
> discussing the same topic with plant managers while I am there.
>
>       There going to be a conference called "The Future of Fashion" in October of this year. I
>
> will attend that conference, and I hope to take at least one designer with me. I going to ask
>
> 10 all of you to vote at the beginning of September for the designer you think deserves to go.

# Self-Assessment

Circle the word or phrase that correctly completes each sentence.

1. My sister thinks her son Billy _____ by the time he's three years old, because she plays the DVD called *Wake Up Your Child's Inner Genius* for him every day.

   a. is reading     b. is going to be reading     c. reads

2. There _____ always _____ unexpected consequences with the introduction of new technology.

   a. are . . . going to     b. will . . . be     c. will . . . being

3. Ming _____ a second home near the ocean if he sells his latest smartphone application for a good price.

   a. will buying     b. is going to buy     c. buys

4. Professor Dham predicts that a flying car _____ never _____ widely available at a reasonable price.

   a. is . . . being     b. is . . . going to be     c. will . . . being

5. That "Future Technology" conference sounds really interesting. I think I _____ to arrange my schedule so I can go with you.

   a. 'm going to be trying     b. 'll try     c. try

6. *Technology Buzz Magazine* says that a car that does not need anyone to drive it _____ available in 2040.

   a. is      b. is being      c. will be

7. My grandmother and her friends really enjoy using social networking sites. The retirement community my grandmother lives in _____ a wireless network very soon.

   a. going to install      b. installs      c. is going to be installing

8. My information technology class starts next week. It _____ on Tuesdays from 1:00 to 2:50.

   a. will meeting      b. are meeting      c. meets

9. CostLess Corporation has agreed that it _____ $20,000,000 to the Remedies Company in order to build three new offices.

   a. will pay      b. pays      c. going to pay

10. Ramesh won't be able to meet with us next Wednesday. He _____ presentations on how to store and analyze data every day for the whole week.

    a. will be giving      b. will give      c. gives

11. Reality Tech Company _____ some exciting new products. Anyone who wants to stay on the cutting edge of technology will like them all.

    a. will adding      b. going to add      c. will be adding

12. The technological changes we have been experiencing will definitely lead to important social changes. However, I don't think everyone _____ able to make the necessary personal changes.

    a. is being      b. going to be      c. will be

13. At 3:00 this Friday, my roommate Pierre _____ a presentation about how new technology has affected online education.

    a. give      b. going to give      c. is going to give

14. The Advisory Committee _____ its findings next Saturday in Deccan Hall.

    a. going to be presenting      b. is presenting      c. will presenting

15. I think the company _____ more people in the fall, but I'm not absolutely sure.

    a. is probably hiring      b. will probably be hiring      c. going to hire

# UNIT 6

## Future Time Clauses, Future Perfect, and Future Perfect Progressive

### Business Practices of the Future

---

## Future Time Clauses

**1** Complete the sentences about Meg, who is going to start an online company selling hats. Use future time clauses with the information in the chart. Sometimes more than one answer is possible.

| 1st Event | 2nd Event |
|---|---|
| 1.  she / find a web designer | Meg / set up her website |
| 2.  the website / be ready | she / post pictures of her products |
| 3.  her customers / place a lot of orders | she / make more hats |
| 4.  she / receive a large order of hats | she / buy more materials |
| 5.  she / finish the hats | she / mail hats to customers |
| 6.  her business / make a profit | she / hire employees and an accountant |
| 7.  she / join an online networking site for entrepreneurs.[1] | the holiday season / arrive |

1. _Meg will set up her website_ as soon as _she finds a web designer._ OR _she has found a web designer._ _____

2. Once _____ ,
   _____ .

3. _____ not _____ until
   _____ .

4. As soon as _____ ,
   _____ .

5. _____ after
   _____ .

6. _____ not _____ until
   _____ .

7. Before _____ ,
   _____ .

---

[1]**entrepreneur:** someone who starts his or her own business, especially when this involves a new opportunity or risk

**2** Complete the e-mail from a small business owner. Use *be going to* or the present perfect form of the verbs in parentheses.

Dear employees:

As you know, our small catering[1] business will expand in January. Please review this list of changes.

1. We will become partners with the company Dessert Delights. Once the companies _*have joined*_ (join) together, we _*are going to offer*_ (offer) their desserts along with our menu for all of our events.

2. We will use a cloud computing service. Once we _____ (install) the system, your work schedules _____ (be) online.

3. We are going paperless next year! We _____ (send) bills by e-mail as soon as the new year _____ (start).

4. We will stop using paper products to serve food. Workers _____ (wash) more dishes after events _____ (end).

5. These changes _____ (not happen) until the new year _____ (begin). There will be a meeting soon to discuss these changes.

[1]**cater:** provide food and drinks for special events

**3** Complete the sentences about future events. Circle the correct form of the verbs.

1. Tina **is going to work** / **works** from home next year three days a week while her husband **is taking** / **will take** care of their children.

2. Next month, Charlotte and Sandra **are going to take / take** online orders for their business while they **are going to remodel / remodel** their store.

3. Denise and Andrew **are already planning / will already be planning** their new restaurant when the loan **comes / will come** through.

4. Dev **is meeting / will be meeting** with programmers about the computer problems when his business partner **arrives / is arriving** from Dubai.

5. Mia **is / is going to be** very careful with her money when her brand-new company **is starting / is going to be starting** up.

6. Next week, Tyrone **interviews / will be interviewing** salespeople while his business partner **is going to plan / is planning** the budget.

**4** Complete the sentences about future events. Write sentences that are true for you.

1. When I finish this class, _____ .

2. While I am taking English classes, I _____ .

3. I _____ until I finish all of my English classes.

4. Once I _____ , I will _____ .

# Future Perfect vs. Future Perfect Progressive

**1** Complete the web article about a corporation's ideas for the future of business in 2020. Use the future perfect form of the verbs in parentheses.

- Many businesses _will have adopted_ (adopt) "green" practices. For example, more
  (1)

  offices _____ (become) very energy-efficient.
  (2)

- The cost of starting a small business _____ (decrease), and
  (3)

  more women _____ (start) their own businesses.
  (4)

- Global markets _____ (become) more interconnected.
  (5)

- Most companies _____ (hire) people to post comments on
  (6)

  social networking sites as a way to advertise their businesses.

- Many more workers _____ (take) jobs as contract employees
  (7)

  who work with different employers for certain periods of time.

**2** Look at the chart with milestones[1] for the Gray & Taylor Company. Write sentences with *by* and the future perfect progressive.

| Month | Who | Activity | Time |
|-------|-----|----------|------|
| 1. January | the company | operate | 100 years |
| 2. March | the director | work at the company | 25 years |
| 3. August | the sales reps | telecommute[2] | 5 years |
| 4. October | the employees | use software to set up meetings | 3 years |

1. _By January, the company will have been operating for 100 years._

2. _____

3. _____

4. _____

[1]**milestone:** important event | [2]**telecommute:** work for a company from home and communicate with the office by computer and telephone

**3** Complete the article from a student alumni newsletter. Circle the correct verb forms.

### What Are People from the Class of 2007 Doing Now?

*Amanda Rogers* will start her own business next year designing websites. By the time she

opens her business, she (**will have completed**) / **will have been completing** a degree in web
                                    (1)

design, and she **will have designed** / **will have been designing** websites for five years. If you
                          (2)

need a good website designer, contact Amanda at arogers7@cambridge.org.

*Rafael Martinez* and *Anne Rosati* will have been married for seven years in June. Their bakery,

Artful Cakes, **will have created** / **will have been creating** amazing-looking cakes for five years by
                        (3)

that time. They **will have baked** / **will have been baking** more than 100,000 cakes by then! Look
                        (4)

for them at www.artfulcakes.cambridge.org, and order one for your next special event.

*Keith Chen* has been offered a job as a computer technician at a large corporation in Guadalajara,

Mexico. He **will have moved** / **will have been moving** to Mexico by the end of the summer. By then,
                    (5)

he **will have studied** / **will have been studying** Spanish at a local language school for at least a few
                (6)

months. He is looking forward to the challenge of working in another country.

# Avoid Common Mistakes

**1** Circle the mistakes.

1. We will interview at least 10 candidates before we **hire** anyone. After I **interview** the
                                                        (a)                              (b)

   candidates, Jo will, too. Once we (**will make**) a decision, we will notify the candidates.
                                          (c)

2. In May, Tanya **will have been studied** nursing for four years. When she graduates, she
                          (a)

   **will have been working** at the clinic for two years. She **will probably get** a promotion.
              (b)                                                    (c)

3. We **will have completed** our business plan before the end of the week. By next month,
              (a)

   our financial advisor **have reviewed** it. By next May, we **will have opened** our business.
                                (b)                                    (c)

4. In June, Luke and his wife **will have worked** for Dr. Lee for four years. In July, he
                                    (a)

   **have been** a nurse for six years, and she **will have been working** as one for five years.
        (b)                                              (c)

5. By 2025, people **will have been used** the Internet for over 45 years. Businesses
                          (a)

   **will have been using** e-mail for over 30 years, and they **will have been working** with
              (b)                                                    (c)

   computers for even longer.

6. John is going to update his office when he **returns** from vacation. When he **will create**
   <sub>(a)</sub> <sub>(b)</sub>

   new systems, he'll train the staff. They **will learn** the systems quickly.
   <sub>(c)</sub>

7. By 2050, business **will have changed** dramatically. Technology **improved** a lot by then.
   <sub>(a)</sub> <sub>(b)</sub>

   People **will have invented** things we can't even imagine now.
   <sub>(c)</sub>

8. My sister **finished** college by the time she is 21. I'm sure that, one year later, she
   <sub>(a)</sub>

   **will have gotten** her first job, and she **will have moved** to her own apartment.
   <sub>(b)</sub> <sub>(c)</sub>

**2** Find and correct eight more mistakes in the paragraph about a new business.

> Ana Ray will start a new child-care center after she ~~will get~~ a child-care license. Once
> she will get the license, she will remodel her home. By next fall, she have turned the first
> floor into a child-care center. By then, her family moved to the second floor. By the time
> the center will have opened, Ana will have been worked with children for 10 years. She
> will be working by herself when she first will open her business, but she may expand. By
> this time next year, she has decided whether an expansion is possible. She have made
> many contacts by then, so she will be able to find many customers.

*gets* (written above "will get")

# Self-Assessment

Circle the word or phrase that correctly completes each sentence.

1. Tomas _____ his degree by the time I see him.

   a. completes      b. will have completed      c. is going to completed

2. Manuel is going to develop new software once he _____ his job.

   a. starts      b. will start      c. started

3. Employees _____ to work on the new computer system until it is thoroughly tested.

   a. won't start      b. will start      c. starts

4. The company _____ cloud computing as soon as the system is running.

   a. is going to use      b. use      c. has been using

5. Tracey will be installing the new computer system _____ the employees are on vacation.

   a. during      b. when      c. until

6. The employees are going to work from home _____ workers are remodeling the office.

    a. while       b. until       c. before

7. We'll be having a conference when the president _____ .

    a. arrived       b. will be arriving       c. arrives

8. By 2020, I _____ here for a decade.

    a. have worked       b. will work       c. will have worked

9. In January, we _____ the new security system for a year.

    a. will use       b. will have been used       c. will have been using

10. By the end of the week, how long will you _____ to get a new computer?

    a. wait       b. have been waiting       c. have been waited

11. Fei will have created a new website _____ the time her business opens.

    a. after       b. once       c. by

12. Keith _____ the manager of this office by this time next year.

    a. has become       b. becomes       c. will have become

13. I'll have _____ been working here for 10 years by the time the new computers are installed.

    a. as soon as       b. already       c. before

14. By this time next week, everyone _____ the news about the company moving.

    a. will have been hearing       b. will have heard       c. heard

15. How long _____ your computer when the new model comes out?

    a. will you have had       b. will you have been having       c. are you having

# Social Modals

## Learning How to Remember

# Modals and Modal-like Expressions of Advice and Regret

**1** Complete the conversation about advice for helping older people with memory and cognitive problems. Circle the correct modals or modal-like expressions.

**Ada:** This article has some great advice on how to help

older people with memory and cognitive problems.

**Jia:** What type of advice do they give?

**Ada:** Well, for instance, they say you (should)/ had better
(1)

be patient. It's not the person's fault if he or she can't

remember something.

**Jia:** That's a little obvious, isn't it?

**Ada:** They also say that you **ought / should** help the person
(2)

create a regular routine. A regular schedule helps a person be less confused.

**Jia:** Hmm. I'd never thought of that.

**Ada:** And you **'d better not / could** schedule difficult activities, like doctor's appointments,
(3)

in the afternoon.

**Jia:** Why not?

**Ada:** They say that people with memory and cognitive problems are often more anxious

later in the day.

**Jia:** Oh. I once heard that you **might not / could not** want to give them a lot of choices. It
(4)

seems that people with these problems deal better with fewer options. There's less to

have to think about and analyze that way.

**Ada:** Oh, that's interesting. They also say that you **should not / might not** have a lot of
(5)

noise in your home if the person lives with you. For example, if people are talking,

make sure the TV is off.

**Jia:** Uh-oh. I would have a hard time remembering to do that.

**Ada:** And another thing that experts say is that if the person's problems become more serious, you **'d better / could not** get professional help from doctors and nurses. They
(6)

say you **should not / ought** deal with them on your own.
(7)

**Jia:** This is all good advice. It sounds as if the article was really worth reading. Can I

borrow it from you?

**2** Complete the paragraph with advice about how to remember things. Use *could*, *had better*, *might*, *ought to*, or *should*. Use negative forms when appropriate. Sometimes more than one answer is possible. Use each modal at least once.

To help you remember information, you _*should*_ divide it into small chunks. For
(1)

example, you _____ divide a phone number into several small parts.
(2)

You _____ remember it as 256-555-69-09 instead of 2565556909.
(3)

Another way to remember things is to associate something with the first letter of the

words you want to remember. For this method, you _____ write
(4)

down the words you want to remember. For example, if you are trying to remember your

classmates' names, write down their names and circle the first letter of each name. For

example, Ⓑethany, Ⓜarcos, Ⓢamantha, and so on. Then you _____
(5)

think of something that starts with each letter and associate it with the person. "Blue"

starts with "b," and Bethany has blue eyes. "Messy" starts with "m," and Marcos is messy.

"Smart" starts with "s," and Samantha is very smart. You _____ start
(6)

with a long list, or you will find the task too difficult. You _____
(7)

memorize a few names at a time, and then add a few more. Soon you'll discover that you

know everyone's names and you'll have a great new memorization trick!

**3** Read the sentences about people who forgot or didn't do important things. Then give your opinion. Write one sentence with *should have* and one sentence with *shouldn't have*.

1. Jared forgot his teacher's name. He called her by the wrong name.

   *He shouldn't have forgotten her name. He should have written it down.*

2. Laura missed some English classes, so she didn't have any notes to study for the test. She didn't do well on her test.

   _____

3. Alison never writes down her homework assignments. Last night, she forgot to do her homework.

   _____

4. Charles had to give a speech for his class. He didn't practice it, and he couldn't remember everything he wanted to say.

   _____

# Modals and Modal-like Expressions of Permission, Necessity, and Obligation

**1** Complete the advertisement and list of rules for a memory experiment. Circle the correct modals or modal-like expressions.

---

**Memory Tests at the Memory Lab**

The Memory Lab is conducting research on how knowing more than one language affects memory. You **must** / **must not** meet the following requirements to
                                                    (1)
participate.

- You **must** / **aren't supposed to** know two or more languages. One of the
                      (2)
  languages **has to** / **doesn't have to** be English because the test is in English.
                      (3)
- You need to be able to speak, read, and write the second language, but you

  **are allowed to** / **don't have to** use it regularly. As long as you know it, it doesn't
                      (4)
  matter how much you actually use it.

- For this test, you **are required to** / **must not** be at least 21 years old. We will not
                      (5)
  accept participants under the age of 21.

---

---

**Test Rules**

---

Thank you for participating in the Memory Lab study. Please follow these test rules.

- You **were supposed to / must not** bring your ID with you. If the test administrator (6) has not asked for it yet, please show it to him or her before you take the test.

- You **were not required to / were not supposed to** bring food or drink into the test (7) area. If you have it with you, please throw it away now.

- You cannot talk to the other participants during the test. If the test administrator finds you talking to anyone, you **will have to / aren't supposed to** leave the testing (8) area immediately.

- You **are required to / don't have to** stay for the entire time. If you finish the test early, (9) please wait until the hour is over. The test administrator will tell you when to leave.

**2 A** Look at the rules for things that students are allowed and not allowed to do during a test. Write sentences with *can*, *can't*, *may*, or *may not*. Sometimes more than one answer is possible.

| Test Rules | Allowed | Not Allowed |
|---|---|---|
| 1. Talk to your classmates. | | ✔ |
| 2. Talk to the teacher. | ✔ | |
| 3. Ask the teacher for help with directions. | ✔ | |
| 4. Use your notes. | | ✔ |
| 5. Use a dictionary. | ✔ | |
| 6. Have your textbooks open. | | ✔ |

1. *You can't talk to your classmates.* OR *You may not talk to your classmates.*

2. _____

3. _____

4. _____

5. _____

6. _____

**B** Complete the conversation with the past form of the modals and modal-like expressions in parentheses. Use the test rules from A.

**Drew:** How was your test today, Kate?

**Kate:** It was really hard. We _couldn't use_ (cannot / use) our
(1)
notes.

**Drew:** Really? _____ (can / you / use)
(2)
a dictionary?

**Kate:** Yes. And we _____ (be allowed to / ask) the teacher
(3)
for help with directions.

**Drew:** That's good. Hey, do you want to work on our science project now? Did you bring
your laptop?

**Kate:** Oh, no. We _____ (not be allowed to / bring)
(4)
laptops to class today. I left it at home.

**Drew:** Let's go to the library and use the computers there. By the way, where is your
textbook? Did you forget to bring it with you?

**Kate:** Oh, we _____ (cannot / open) our textbooks during the
(5)
test, so I left it in my car.

**Drew:** That was a good idea. Well, I'm sure you did well on the test.

**Kate:** I think so. But I got in trouble with Professor Jenkins, and I was really embarrassed.
We _____ (not be allowed to / talk) during
(6)
the test, and I asked Luis a question. I felt awful!

**Drew:** That's too bad.

**Kate:** I know . . . and I was only asking him what time it was!

# Modals and Modal-like Expressions of Ability

**1** Correct the mistakes in bold in the article about photographic memory.

                                     *is able to remember*

Photographic memory occurs when a person **is able remember** a large amount of information accurately. Experts disagree on whether or not a person **can to have** a photographic memory. Some experts say it is extremely rare. They say that some children **are able to remembering** a lot of information. However, as adults, they **not able to do**

5  this. Other experts say that photographic memory does not exist.

Many people think that a photographic memory would be wonderful. Some researchers say this is not true. When people have photographic memory, they **are able store** a great deal of information, like a computer database. However, they might remember a lot of information that is not necessary for everyday life. Researchers

10  say that memory is only important when people **can used** it in their everyday lives. If people remember everything they see, read, and hear, they **will be not able to organize** the information in a useful way and recall it quickly when they need it. Also, sometimes people with photographic memory **can forget not** things they don't want to remember.

Some experts say that photographic memory is not something people are born with.

15  They believe that people who **can to remember** large amounts of information have to work hard so that they **can to do** this.

**2** Write sentences with the present or past form of the modals and modal-like expressions.

1. Some people say that the composer Wolfgang Amadeus Mozart had a fantastic memory for music.

   They say he / can / play / very long and complex pieces of music from memory

   *They say he could play very long and complex pieces of music from memory.*

2. Most musicians playing Mozart's compositions nowadays don't have such extraordinary memory.

   However, they / be able to / memorize / his pieces by practicing a lot

   _____

3. Solomon Shereshevsky was a Russian journalist who never took notes during meetings.

   His editor / cannot / understand / how / Shereshevsky / be able to remember / everything he heard

   _____

4. Dr. Luria, who studied memory and the brain, gave Shereshevsky memory tests.

   The journalist / be able to / remember / a long list of numbers

   _____

5. Many students want to remember things as easily as Shereshevsky did.

   However, most students / not be able to / remember / information without studying

   _____

**3** Complete the sentences about memory in the classroom. Use *could have* or *couldn't have* with the correct form of the verbs in parentheses.

1. Ms. Brooks *couldn't have remembered* (remember) all of her students' names. She had too many students.

2. Sandra _____ (learn) all of her classmates' names, but she didn't take the trouble to do it.

3. Elena _____ (get) a better score on the language test, but she was too nervous to remember what she had learned.

4. Jen and Mark _____ (give) their presentation today. Mark was sick and didn't come to class.

5. I _____ (read) Mozart's music diary like the teacher asked us to. I don't understand German!

6. I _____ (pass) the math test even though I spent weeks studying for it. I just don't understand the basic ideas.

# Avoid Common Mistakes

**1** Circle the mistakes.

1. You **shouldn't have stayed up** late studying the night before the test. You
   (a)
   (should studied) the week before the test. Good students **are supposed to know** such
   (b)                                                                    (c)
   basic study rules.

2. **I could studied** more last night, but I went to the movies. **I should have stayed** home!
   (a)                                                                    (b)
   I hope **I will be allowed** to retake the test if I don't do well on it.
   (c)

3. My sister **could have been** badly hurt in the accident, but she had her seat belt on.
   (a)
   She **can't remember** the accident, but she didn't lose the rest of her memory.
   (b)
   I **supposed to be** with her that day, but I decided to stay home.
   (c)

4. My friend **was able to get** her documentary movie about memory problems into a
   (a)
   festival. She **must not have paid** to enter it, but she **could have donated** money to the
   (b)                                        (c)
   film organization if she wanted to.

5. You **should have called** me for advice. You **should backed up** your computer. Now,
   (a)                                    (b)
   you **should buy** an external drive with a lot of memory or get a subscription to an
   (c)
   online backup site.

6. The test rules were OK. We **didn't have to worry** about spelling for the test because
   (a)
   we could use dictionaries. However, we **had to memorize** the important facts because
   (b)
   we couldn't use our books. But the best rule was that we **must not have stayed** for the
   (c)
   entire class if we finished the test early. It's so boring when you have to sit there waiting

   for everybody to finish.

7. Mr. Lin **is supposed to give** us our final assignment today. We **supposed to work**
   (a)                                                            (b)
   alone. We **aren't allowed to copy** information from other people.
   (c)

8. You **should remembered** the teaching assistant's name. You **should have asked** a
   (a)                                                            (b)
   classmate if you **couldn't remember** it.
   (c)

**2** Find and correct eight more mistakes in the article about an experiment on memory.

---

**Cats and Memory: An Experiment**

     *was*
Anne Park ∧supposed to create an experiment to test the memories of cats. She

developed the following test. She put a block between a cat and a treat. The cat allowed

to get the treat, but the block was in the way. The first time the cat tried to get the treat, it

5 tripped over the block. The second time, it remembered the block was there and stepped

over it. Anne then played with the cat in another room and then repeated the experiment.

Each time she played with the cat a little bit longer. The cat remembered the block was

there for up to 10 minutes. After 10 minutes of play, the cat tripped over the block. Anne

was surprised. She thought the cat should remembered the block.

     Anne concluded that cats have memories of about 10 minutes. She must not have

10 turned in her results right away, so she decided to test her theory with more cats. She

borrowed 10 cats from a shelter and repeated the experiment. She allowed to keep the

cats for several days. The results were the same. Anne's boss thought the results were

successful, but she had some criticisms. She thought that Anne should tested even more

cats for her experiment. She also thought Anne's notes should included more details.

15      Anne supposed to return the cats to the shelter. She must not have found homes for

the cats, but she wanted to.

---

# Self-Assessment

Circle the word or phrase that correctly completes each sentence.

1. You _____ try using flash cards to memorize new vocabulary. It really helped me.

    a. ought to     b. aren't allowed to     c. should have

2. Carlos _____ miss class. If he does, he might not pass.

    a. could have     b. shouldn't     c. has to

3. Erica _____ study for the test next week. She didn't do very well on the last test.

    a. had better     b. might not want to     c. is allowed to

4. You _____ memorize all of the vocabulary because we can use our books during the test.

    a. might not want to    b. might    c. are required to

5. Jake _____ be a part of the memory study because he's not old enough.

    a. may    b. is permitted to    c. can't

6. Are we _____ tell people about the research project?

    a. must    b. allowed to    c. can

7. Isabel _____ 100 questions for the English grammar test. She hopes she has time to finish them all.

    a. must    b. must answer    c. must have answered

8. Were you _____ your memory test yesterday morning?

    a. supposed to schedule    b. mustn't schedule    c. could have scheduled

9. The students _____ turn in their cell phones before they could take the test.

    a. must not    b. didn't have    c. had to

10. The doctor _____ give good advice on how to help patients who have problems concentrating or remembering things.

    a. shouldn't    b. could have    c. was able to

11. Cats have short-term memory, and they _____ remember most things for more than 10 minutes.

    a. aren't able to    b. mustn't    c. didn't have to

12. Fish _____ remember smells.

    a. are able to    b. are able    c. are allowed to

13. Elephants _____ survive in the wild because they have good memories.

    a. are required to    b. are permitted to    c. can

14. You _____ me the test was canceled. You knew I had missed the last class.

    a. won't tell    b. should have told    c. could tell

15. Jun _____ tested my photographic memory. I wouldn't let him.

    a. had to    b. should have    c. couldn't have

# Modals of Probability:
# Present, Future, and Past

## Computers and Crime

---

## Modals of Present Probability

**1** Read the web article about creating strong passwords. Then read the passwords and the writer's opinion about them. Circle the correct modals to complete the sentences.

### Stronger Passwords, Better Security

Follow these suggestions to create a strong password. A good password is one that is easy for you to remember but hard for someone else to guess.

- Make your password at least five characters long.
- Use a combination of letters and numbers.
- Don't use letters in alphabetical order, like ABCDE or MNOPQRS.
- Don't use your birth date or phone number as part of the password.
- You can use a foreign word, like your favorite color in German.

| Password | Opinion |
|----------|---------|
| 1. 569652 | This password contains only numbers. Because there are no letters, it **shouldn't /(can't)/ may not** be a good password. The person definitely needs a different password. |
| 2. Sept71992jb | This **couldn't / may not / shouldn't** be a good password. It contains a date, which could be the person's birthday. The person probably needs a different password. |
| 3. blooppa | This password is a made-up word. That's fine, but it doesn't contain numbers. This **shouldn't / has to / might not** be a good password because it does not have numbers. |
| 4. anaranjado629 | This password contains a foreign word. It means "orange" in Spanish. The password also includes numbers. This **should / could / may** be a good password because it fits all of the suggestions. |
| 5. 346b | This password is only four characters long. It is too short, so it **couldn't / might not / shouldn't** be a good password. |
| 6. tyn80oh42 | This password is over five characters long, it contains numbers and letters, and it is very difficult for someone to guess. It's perfect! This **has to / may / might** be a good password. |
| 7. 49bcde1r | This password contains a combination of letters and numbers, but it also has some letters in alphabetical order. Still, it's probably OK. This **might / must / has to** be a good password. |

**2** Complete the conversation about hacking with the correct modals. Use the words in parentheses to help you. Sometimes more than one answer is possible.

**Dana:** Who do you think is hacking into our computer system?

**Samir:** I don't know. It <u>*could / may / might*</u> (unsure) be

(1)

professional hackers. They steal credit card numbers

and other kinds of ID numbers because sometimes they

can make a lot of money from the stolen information.

**Dana:** Or it _____ (unsure) be an

(2)

ex-employee. Some ex-employees who are angry with their old employer try to

make trouble for the company. Sometimes they delete information from computer

systems or even shut down the systems.

**Samir:** No way! It _____ (not possible) be an ex-employee. All our

(3)

employees seem to be honest people. It _____ (a logical

(4)

conclusion) be a professional hacker. It _____ (not possible)

(5)

be anyone we know!

**Dana:** Well, it _____ (unsure) be someone from outside the

(6)

company. But the company _____ (expectation based

(7)

on evidence) be able to find out who did it pretty quickly. We have a good tech

department.

**Samir:** I know, the company _____ (a logical conclusion) have a way

(8)

to see who is doing it.

**Dana:** You're right, and they _____ (a logical conclusion) know how

(9)

to fix the problems it's causing. That's their job.

# Modals of Future Probability

**1 A** Javier's company is paying for him to take classes for a certificate in computer security. He has written notes about the classes he plans to take. Read his notes. Then complete the sentences with modals of future probability and the verbs in parentheses. Use *will* (*not*) for strong certainty, *should* (*not*) for certainty, or *might* (*not*) for less certainty. Sometimes more than one answer is possible.

| Required courses: | |
| --- | --- |
| IS 101: Information Security Basics | Definitely spring semester this year. |
| IS 201: Advanced Information Security | Probably fall semester this year or spring next year. |
| **Optional courses (must take 3):** | |
| IS 102: Internet Security Issues | Probably fall semester this year. |
| ~~IS 202: Internet Privacy Issues~~ | I've taken a course like this already. |
| IS 103: Forensic Computer Science | Possibly this summer. If not, next summer. |
| ~~IS 104: Software Security~~ | I prefer to take other courses. |
| IS 204: Network Security | Probably spring next year. |

Javier _will take_ (take) classes to get a certificate in Information Systems Security.
(1)

His company _____ (pay) for all of the classes, so luckily he
(2)

_____ (not spend) any of his own money.
(3)

He probably _____ (not finish) the certificate this year because
(4)

he has to work at the same time. He _____ (get) it next year.
(5)

He _____ (take) the first required course this spring.
(6)

He _____ (not be) in school during the summer this year. After
(7)

he finishes IS 101, he _____ (know) whether he is going to take
(8)

IS 201 this fall semester. If he doesn't take it then, he _____ (be)
(9)

ready to take it next spring. He _____ (not take) the class IS 202
(10)

because he has already taken a similar course. He _____ (finish)
(11)

taking classes next year.

**B** Nicole works at the same company as Javier. Read her notes and write sentences about them. Use modals of future probability and the progressive form of the verbs. Sometimes more than one answer is possible.

> – Take summer classes from June–August, already registered and paid for
> – Finish degree in information security, must pass summer courses
> – Probably graduate January 4 if I take a fall class
> – Hope to get a promotion in January; not looking for a new job even if I don't get the promotion

1. take a vacation in June

   *Nicole won't be taking a vacation in June.*

2. take classes in the summer

   _____

3. take a class in the fall

   _____

4. graduate in January

   _____

5. get a promotion in January

   _____

6. look for a new job in January

   _____

**2** Answer the questions with modals of future probability. Write sentences that are true for you.

1. Will you take classes to learn about computer security?

   _____

2. Will you change your e-mail password in the next month?

   _____

3. Will you pay your bills online this year?

   _____

4. Will you update the antivirus software of your computer in the next year?

   _____

5. Will you buy a new computer in the next year?

   _____

# Modals of Past Probability

**1** Circle the sentence in each pair that expresses greater certainty.

1. a. Scott must have read the book *Computers, Crime, and You.*

   b. Scott might have read the book *Computers, Crime, and You.*

2. a. He may not have learned anything from the book, though.

   b. He couldn't have learned anything from the book, though.

3. a. He must not have followed the tips in the book, because he had a problem with his computer.

   b. He might not have followed the tips in the book, because he had a problem with his computer.

4. a. Someone could have hacked into his computer last week.

   b. Someone must have hacked into his computer last week.

5. a. The problem could not have been very serious, because he fixed his computer pretty quickly.

   b. The problem might not have been very serious, because he fixed his computer pretty quickly.

6. a. Someone might have helped him, though.

   b. Someone must have helped him, though.

**2** Read the information about different kinds of hackers. Then read the descriptions of people. Say what kind of hackers they probably were and guess what they did. Use *must have* if you are sure. Use *could have* or *may have* if you are not sure or if you are guessing. Sometimes more than one answer is possible.

> ## Kinds of Computer Hackers
>
> **A black hat hacker:**  Someone who breaks into computer systems to steal information such as passwords, credit card numbers, and bank information.
>
> **A white hat hacker:**  Someone who breaks into a computer system legally. For example, a company might hire someone to hack into their computers to test their security system.
>
> **A phreaker:**  Someone who hacks into a telecommunications system. For example, a person may hack into a phone company's system so that he or she can send free text messages.
>
> **A hobby hacker:**  Someone who hacks into computers for fun. This person might try to change a program at home for himself or herself.

1. Dustin didn't like paying for text messages. On his latest phone bill, the phone company didn't charge him for any texts, even though he sent a lot of them.

   *Dustin must have been a phreaker. He may have hacked into the phone*
   *company's system.*

2. Silvia bought a lot of items using other people's money. She was arrested last week.

   _____

3. Debbie worked for a large computer company. The company paid her to break into their computers.

   _____

4. Claire borrowed a computer program from a friend. She didn't have the code to use it, but she hacked into it and copied it onto her computer.

   _____

5. Carl figured out a way that he could make free phone calls. The phone company caught him.

   _____

# Avoid Common Mistakes

**1** Circle the mistakes.

1. **Ben must working** for that new computer company. **He could work** in the IT
   (a)                                                   (b)
   department, or **he might be developing** security software.
   (c)

2. Limei **will give** a presentation at a conference on computer crimes next week. The
   (a)
   presentation **must be** about computer safety. She **will meet** with some of our clients.
   (b)                                                  (c)

3. Josh **might have lost** some important computer files. He **may have not backed up** all
   (a)                                                        (b)
   of his files. A virus **could have gotten** into his system and destroyed them.
   (c)

4. I **could finishing** my degree next year. I **may be getting** a promotion when I'm done. If
   (a)                                           (b)
   this happens, I **will be celebrating** with my family!
   (c)

5. It **will be** difficult to prove Heather is the hacker. The company **won't say** it is her unless
   (a)                                                                  (b)
   they are certain. They **must not find out** if she did it because they probably will not find
   (c)
   any proof.

6. People **might not getting** as much junk mail in the future. Computer programmers
   (a)
   **may figure out** how to stop junk mail. This **will help** solve problems with e-mail scams.
   (b)                                              (c)

7. More universities **may be offering** computer science degrees to their students in the
   (a)
   future. More IT people **might be learning** about computer security. Hopefully, hackers
   (b)
   **must not be learning** about it, too!
   (c)

8. **Anyone could have hacked** into your computer. **Could someone have guessed** your
   (a)                                              (b)
   password? **You might have not created** a good password.
   (c)

**2** Find and correct eight more mistakes in the paragraphs about a woman's potential new job.

---

**Erin's New Job?**

     be
Erin might ∧ getting a job as a white hat hacker for a large computer company. She

may working with one or two other people to test the system. The hackers will try to find

weaknesses in the system. Erin thinks that she must enjoy this type of work if she gets

the job. She might starting the job in the next few weeks.

5  If Erin does get the job, she won't fixing the problems. Instead, she must be preparing

a report to the company. Someone else will fix the problems because Erin doesn't have

the experience to do that. She is upset that she cannot fix problems as well because she

would make more money. Unfortunately, she could have not gotten a degree in software

development because her college didn't offer software development classes. Instead, she

10 studied computer security systems.

  Erin might have not gotten other jobs she applied for, but that's OK. She's really

hopeful about her chances for this job. If she gets the job and does well, maybe she must

go back to school once she's making more money.

---

# Self-Assessment

Circle the word or phrase that correctly completes each sentence.

1. Jim _____ be a computer hacker. He doesn't know anything about computers, and he
   would never do anything illegal.

   a. can't  b. must  c. might

2. _____ your password be too weak? Maybe that's why someone is getting into your e-mail.

   a. Will  b. Can't  c. Could

3. Mr. Simpson _____ having computer problems. He hasn't responded to my e-mail.

    a. might be        b. might        c. might not

4. It _____ be hard to find a good computer technician because many experienced people have applied.

    a. shouldn't       b. shouldn't have        c. should

5. You _____ have good security software already if your computer is not getting any viruses.

    a. shouldn't       b. can't        c. should

6. Mario _____ start his new job next Wednesday. He'll be working for Computer Plus.

    a. can't       b. will        c. must

7. Rina has to _____ home soon. She only works until 5:00 p.m.

    a. might come        b. be coming        c. coming

8. The new e-mail system _____ running by next week.

    a. must        b. may have        c. should be

9. Greg _____ likely get a degree in systems security. He has applied to the program.

    a. will       b. might        c. won't

10. Employees _____ expect new virus protection software. The company just updated the software last month.

    a. will        b. shouldn't        c. must

11. We probably _____ find out who the hacker is.

    a. won't       b. might        c. may

12. I _____ forgotten my password. It was my first name!

    a. could        b. may have        c. couldn't have

13. She _____ had a strong password. Someone hacked her e-mail.

    a. must have not        b. must not have        c. must not

14. The company _____ hired Peng. I'm not sure.

    a. can't have        b. might have        c. must have

15. You _____ gotten the e-mail about the computer problem. The tech department in the office sent it yesterday.

    a. have to        b. can't have        c. must have

# Nouns and Modifying Nouns

## Attitudes Toward Nutrition

## Nouns

**1** Rewrite the sentences about healthy lifestyles. Change the singular nouns in bold to plural nouns. Change the plural nouns in bold to singular nouns. Change the determiners to the words in parentheses. Change the verbs when necessary.

1. You should eat **a vegetable** every day. (three)

   *You should eat three vegetables every day.*

2. Some experts say it's healthy to get **10 hours** of exercise daily. (an)

   _____

3. Some people need to drink **a glass** of water every day. (six)

   _____

4. **Some diets** are too extreme. (that)

   _____

5. You should eat **one meal** a day. (three)

   _____

6. It's OK to have **several snacks** during the day. (a)

   _____

7. **All children** need to have a diet with enough calcium to build bones. (a)

   _____

8. It is healthy to add **a strawberry** to your cereal. (some)

   _____

**2** Complete the paragraphs about fad diets. Circle the correct words.

A fad diet is a diet that is very popular and then disappears. In one fad diet, the dieter

ate mostly (cabbage)/ cabbages and fruit. People on this diet cooked the cabbage with
          (1)

**onion / onions**, **water / waters**, and **salt / salts**. The **soup / soups** made from this recipe
  (2)         (3)        (4)       (5)

was bad-tasting. Often, those on this **diet / diets** did lose some **weight / weights**.
<sub>(6)</sub> <sub>(7)</sub>

However, this **loss / losses** mostly came from poor **nutrition / nutritions**. People would
<sub>(8)</sub> <sub>(9)</sub>

quickly gain back pounds once they stopped following the diet. It is certainly true that

**vegetable / vegetables** like cabbage are part of a healthy diet plan. However, on their
<sub>(10)</sub>

own, they may not provide all the nutrients people need for good **health / healths**.
<sub>(11)</sub>

Look at the websites of health organizations for good health **advice / advices**.
<sub>(12)</sub>

For example, the American Heart Association website has quite a lot of very good

**information / informations**. It suggests that the most successful plan for most people
<sub>(13)</sub>

is to eat less and to get regular **exercise / exercises**.
<sub>(14)</sub>

**3** Look at the chart. Write sentences about what you can and can't have on this diet. Make the count nouns plural.

| Diet Recommendations | |
|---|---|
| **Allowed** | **Not Allowed** |
| 1. rice | potato |
| 2. chicken | beef |
| 3. fish | pasta |
| 4. nut | cookie |
| 5. bread | donut |
| 6. vegetable | fruit |
| 7. yogurt | egg |
| 8. tea | coffee |

1. *You can have rice. You can't have potatoes.*

2. _____

3. _____

4. _____

5. _____

6. _____

7. _____

8. _____

**4** Rewrite the sentences about health. Use your opinion and *the* + adjective for groups of people.

1. Elderly people need to exercise a lot.

   _____

2. Rich people don't always have a better diet.

   _____

3. Educated people know what kinds of food are healthy.

   _____

4. It can be hard for poor people to have healthy eating habits.

   _____

5. Sick people should exercise regularly.

   _____

# Noncount Nouns as Count Nouns

**1** Complete the sentences about people's likes and habits. Use the singular and plural forms of the words in parentheses. Use each form at least once in each item.

1. I always make *time* for yoga since it's my favorite way to exercise. I take a yoga class three *times* a week. (time)

2. I love _____ ! My favorite _____ are cheddar, Swiss, and feta. (cheese)

3. I don't like to eat red _____ , so I never eat _____ like beef or duck. (meat)

4. My favorite _____ are blueberries and raspberries, but I don't eat _____ very often. (fruit)

5. I drink _____ every morning. I prefer herbal _____ like chamomile and mint. (tea)

6. My favorite _____ are tomato _____ and cream of broccoli. (soup)

7. I like fast _____ a lot, but many fast _____ are unhealthy. (food)

8. I make my own _____ every morning because the _____ in stores have a lot of sugar added. (juice)

**2** Complete the health plan Lisa's nutritionist wrote for her. Circle the correct measurement words.

**Daily Diet and Exercise:**

- Eat about six ounces of grains; at least half of the grains should be

  whole grains.

- Eat (three cups of) / a slice of vegetables and **two cups of / two drops of** fruit.
  (1)                                                              (2)

- Have **a kind of / three cups of** milk or milk products.
  (3)

- Have about half **an article of / a pound of** meat.
  (4)

- Have only **five teaspoons of / a kind of** oil. Please notice that some foods,
  (5)

  like nuts and fish, already contain **a bit of / a slice of** natural oil.
  (6)

- Drink enough water for your individual needs. You don't have to drink

  **eight pinches of / eight glasses of** water.
  (7)

- Do **an hour of / a piece of** exercise every day.
  (8)

**3** Complete Mark's diet and exercise plan with words in the boxes. Use measurement words and a noun for each item.

| Measurement Words | |
| --- | --- |
| a few drops of | a pinch of |
| a game of | ~~a slice of~~ |
| a glass of | two cups of |
| a piece of | two quarts of |

| Nouns | |
| --- | --- |
| basketball | oil |
| ~~bread~~ | salt |
| corn | water |
| milk | watermelon |

**Grains:** _A slice of bread_ and a 1/2 cup of brown rice
      (1)        (1)

**Vegetables:** A cup of spinach and _____ _____
                                   (2)             (2)

**Fruit:** _____ _____ and an orange
         (3)          (3)

**Dairy:** _____ _____ , some yogurt, and two pieces of cheese
        (4)         (4)

**Meat:** Grilled chicken with a little pepper and _____ _____
                                         (5)          (5)

**Oil:** _____ _____ used to grill the chicken
      (6)        (6)

**Water:** _____ _____
        (7)       (7)

**Exercise:** An hour of swimming and _____ _____
                         (8)       (8)

# Modifying Nouns

**1** Unscramble the sentences about a new gym.

1. big / new / a / gym / our town has

   _Our town has a big new gym._

2. rectangular / pool / an / it has / enormous / swimming

   _____

3. exercise / modern / equipment / it has / great

   _____

4. big / weights / metal / there are / round

   _____

5. popular / the gym offers / classes / yoga

   _____

6. new / a / café / the gym has / wonderful / European

   _____

7. bowls of fruit / large / the café serves / delicious

   _____

8. healthy / there are also / in the café / Japanese / teas

   _____

**2** Complete the conversation between a couple shopping for exercise equipment. Put the adjectives in parentheses in the correct order to complete the conversation. Add *and* when necessary.

**Paul:** This new resale shop is really big! We should be able to find the things we need

for our new exercise program. I'm going to look for _large plastic_ (large / plastic)
(1)

dumbbells for exercising.

**Steph:** And I want to go to the clothing department first. I really need to buy a

_____ (cotton / new) T-shirt for exercising. . . .
(2)

**Paul:** Here are some T-shirts. That _____ (blue / white) T-shirt is
(3)

nice. Do you like it?

**Steph:** It's perfect. And look at that _____ (black / great) T-shirt
(4)

with the _____ (red / yellow) writing on it. It looks very
(5)

comfortable.

**Paul:** Hey, look at this _____ (green / purple / ugly) lamp! It's awful!
(6)

**Steph:** Wait! There's a _____ (antique / ceramic / lovely) vase next
(7)

to it. I wonder what it costs.

**Paul:** Hey, don't forget that we're just here for the exercise stuff. But let's go to that

_____ (coffee / French / great) shop on the corner
(8)

after we buy everything. We need and deserve a treat before we start our

_____ (new / exercise / fun) plan. We can have a slice
(9)

of their _____ (strawberry / delicious) tart.[1]
(10)

_____

[1]**tart:** a pastry with a sweet filling and no top

# Avoid Common Mistakes

**1** Circle the mistakes.

1. **A 5-year-old** child should eat one and a half cups of vegetables a day.
(a)
**An 11-year-old girl** should eat two cups. (A 25-years-old man) should eat three cups.
(b)                                                   (c)

2. Livia ate **three slices of pizza** with **different vegetable** on it. She also drank
(a)                                 (b)
**a glass of soda**.
(c)

3. The department of food services **recommend** eating healthy food. Nutritionists **write**
(a)                                                                    (b)
tips on healthy food. Their assistant **updates** the information once a month.
(c)

4. That recipe calls for **two pepper**, **three onions**, and **one carrot**.
(a)          (b)                  (c)

5. The nutrition classes at that university **are** popular. The homework **is** difficult, but the
(a)                                        (b)
students in the program **is** very hardworking.
(c)

6. I'm going to make lemon chicken today. I bought a **32-ounce bottle** of lemon juice, a
(a)
**five-pounds chicken**, and a **one-pound box** of butter for the recipe.
(b)                      (c)

7. My doctor told me that I should drink **eight glasses of waters** every day, try to get
(a)
**an hour of exercise**, and eat **several kinds of vegetables**.
(b)                          (c)

8. The farmer's market has a lot of fresh **fruit**. The **oranges** look good, but the **peach** don't.
(a)                        (b)                    (c)

**2** Find and correct eight more mistakes in the paragraphs about breakfast.

---

**Kids Eat Breakfast**

All ~~meal~~ *meals* are important, but breakfast is the most important meal of the day. It's sometimes hard to get children to eat breakfast. Here is a recipe that children love, and even a five-years-old child can make it! Put food colorings into a three-ounces glass of milk. Use your child's favorite color. Then give your child two slices of breads. Let your child paint a face on each slice with a clean paintbrush and the colored milk. Put the bread into the toaster. Remove it and add some butter. Most child love the fun faces!

Many recipes of this kind is on the KidsEat website. KidsEat is an organization that helps children eat better. The people at the organization is dedicated to improving children's eating habits. The recipe are easy-to-follow and delicious!

---

# Self-Assessment

Circle the word or phrase that correctly completes each sentence.

1. There are several different kinds of _____ in the casserole.

   a. vegetable        b. vegetables        c. a vegetable

2. This recipe requires _____ tomatoes. Do we have any?

   a. the        b. three        c. a

3. I've concluded that _____ is the best exercise for me.

   a. a piece of yoga        b. the yoga        c. yoga

4. _____ is a major problem in the United States.

   a. Obesities        b. The obesity        c. Obesity

5. Do you think there should be food programs to help _____ ?

   a. the poors        b. the poor        c. poor

6. Jackie lost some weight and had to buy new _____ .

   a. pant        b. the pants        c. pants

7. _____ is really delicious.

   a. Italian cheese        b. Some kinds of Italian cheese        c. These Italian cheeses

8. Andrea and Mert had different _____ in the swimming class.

   a. the experience      b. experience      c. experiences

9. Two agencies of the United States Department of Agriculture _____ the Center for Nutrition Policy and Promotion and the Food and Nutrition Service.

   a. is      b. are      c. be

10. How many _____ do you have to move?

    a. furniture      b. pieces of furniture      c. pieces furniture

11. I only put a few _____ of milk in my coffee, and I never use refined sugar.

    a. grains      b. gallons      c. drops

12. My father gave me an _____ maker.

    a. ice-cream, Italian      b. Italian, ice-cream      c. Italian ice-cream

13. I use _____ bag when I shop instead of plastic bags.

    a. an old and cotton      b. an old cotton      c. a cotton old

14. My grandmother has a _____ cake recipe. I'm going to try to make it for the first time!

    a. traditional delicious      b. traditional and delicious      c. delicious traditional

15. Tammy has a _____ table in her kitchen.

    a. metal beautiful new      b. new metal beautiful      c. beautiful new metal

# Articles and Quantifiers

## Color

---

## Indefinite Article, Definite Article, and No Article

**1** Complete the conversation about choosing a color of paint for a room. Use *a / an* or *the*.

**Diana:** Hey, Lucas. I need your help. I want to paint _*a*_ room in my apartment, but
(1)

I don't know what color to paint it.

**Lucas:** What room is it?

**Diana:** It's _____ kitchen.
(2)

**Lucas:** How big is it?

**Diana:** It's _____ really small room. Why?
(3)

**Lucas:** Well, dark colors make _____ room look smaller, and light colors make
(4)

_____ room look bigger.
(5)

**Diana:** Really?

**Lucas:** Yes. Since _____ kitchen is small, you should definitely paint it _____ light
(6)                                                                        (7)

color. How about white?

**Diana:** I don't think so. _____ cupboards are white. I want to add some color.
(8)

**Lucas:** Well, how about _____ pastel yellow? _____ color yellow is cheerful, and it
(9)                                            (10)

will make your kitchen look bigger, too.

**Diana:** You know, that's a good idea.

**2** Complete the sentences about colors with *the* or Ø for no article.

1. Pastels are _Ø_ pale colors. _The_ definition of *pastel* is a very pale or light color.

2. _____ colors _____ light pink, light yellow, and light blue are popular pastel colors.

3. Neon colors are very bright. Flashing signs often use _____ neon colors.

4. _____ pastel blue is a cheerful color that reminds people of _____ sky.

5. Metallic colors are shiny. They look like they have _____ metal in them.

6. Metallic colors such as silver are often used on _____ cars.

**3** Complete the sentences about a color forecaster with *a / an*, *the*, or Ø for no article.

1. Lei is _*a*_ color forecaster.

2. _____ color forecaster predicts what colors will become popular in _____ future.

3. Lei is also _____ interior designer.

4. Lei does _____ research for her job. _____ research helps her determine popular colors.

5. Lei interviews _____ famous people about the best colors for homes.

6. Lei works for _____ company that designs and builds _____ homes.

7. If Lei is right about _____ popularity of a color, the homes built by her company are usually successful.

8. Lei says _____ color Berry Brown is going to become very popular.

9. Lei also thinks Grass Green will be _____ popular color this year.

# Quantifiers

**1** Look at the survey results about favorite colors. Then circle the correct quantifiers in the sentences.

We asked 200 people (100 men and 100 women) what their favorite colors are. Here are the results.

|  | Green | Blue | Brown | Black | Pink | Red | Purple | Orange |
|---|---|---|---|---|---|---|---|---|
| Men | 24 | 37 | 0 | 19 | 0 | 14 | 2 | 4 |
| Women | 12 | 33 | 0 | 2 | 25 | 3 | 25 | 0 |

1. **A great deal of /** (**Many**) **/ No** men liked green, and **no / not much /** (**some**) women liked green.

2. **A few / A little / A lot of** men and women chose blue as their favorite color.

3. **A great deal of / All of / None of** the men and women picked brown.

4. **No / Quite a few / Most** men chose black, but **all / no / not many** women chose black.

5. **A lot of / All / No** women picked pink, but **quite a few / no / not a lot of** men picked it.

6. **A great deal of / All / Some** men chose red, but only **a lot of / a few / no** women chose it.

7. **Many / Not a lot of / Not much** women chose purple, but **a little / many / not a lot of** men chose purple.

8. **A few of / All of / Most of** the men picked orange, but **a few of / not many / none of** the women picked orange.

**2** Complete the paragraphs about a famous painter. Use *a few*, *few*, *a little*, or *little*.

_Few_ painters are as well known as Claude Monet. Monet was born in Paris, France, in
(1)
1840. At the beginning of his career, he had _____ success. In fact, he wasn't
(2)
famous, and he owed people money.

Monet painted some of his most important paintings in the 1870s. He painted

nature, but he only included _____ details. His style was called
(3)
*impressionistic* because it showed his impression of nature, not how things really looked.

_____ artists were painting like this at the time, so Monet's style looked
(4)
unusual and fresh. _____ people started to buy his paintings, and gradually
(5)
he was able to save _____ money. He bought a home at Giverny, northwest
(6)
of Paris, and made a garden. He painted the garden in many of his pictures.

In the 1880s and 1890s, he became successful financially and artistically. Today, there

are _____ people who haven't heard of Monet and his paintings.
(7)

**3** Read the article about how animals see colors. Cross out *of* in the phrases in bold when it is
not correct.

People can see **a lot of** colors, but exactly how many colors can they see? Experts do
(1)
not have an exact answer, but **some ~~of~~** experts say people see about 10 million colors.
(2)
The human eye can detect even **a little of** difference in color – for example, when a
(3)
color is just slightly darker or lighter than another color.

**Not many of** animals see colors the way people do, but **some of** animals do.
(4)                                                                    (5)
**Not much of** research exists to show exactly how many colors animals see, but
(6)
scientists have been able to figure out **a lot of** things. Here are **a few of** fun facts:
(7)                                                      (8)
• Research shows that **quite a few of** insects are attracted to certain colors.
(9)
• Bees can see **many of** shades of color that people cannot see.
(10)
• **Some of** the research shows that dogs and cats only see **a few of** colors.
(11)                                                            (12)
• **Many of** scientists believe whales and dolphins are color blind. These animals can
(13)
see patterns in light, but **no of** colors.
(14)
• **All of** scientists agree on one thing: **a great deal of** research still has to be done.
(15)                                          (16)

# Avoid Common Mistakes

**1** Circle the mistakes.

1. There are (much) trends with hair color. **Many of** the trends involve bright colors. My
       (a)                               (b)

   sister has dyed her hair pink **many** times.
                           (c)

2. **A lot of** my clothes are colorful, and **many of** them are bright colors, but **not much of**
     (a)                          (b)                   (c)

   them are neon.

3. Julie is **assistant** at a paint store, but she wants to be **a color forecaster**. She might get
           (a)                                 (b)

   a job in the field because her father knows **many people** in the paint business.
                                    (c)

4. **A lot of** people use digital cameras. **Not many** people take pictures in black and white,
     (a)                      (b)

   but **alot of** people take pictures in color.
       (c)

5. **Not many of** my friends like the color pink. In addition, **a lot of** them don't like brown.
     (a)                                  (b)

   **Much of** them love black, though.
     (c)

6. Loretta is **photographer**, but she has been working part-time as **a photo researcher**
            (a)                                 (b)

   because she doesn't have **a lot of** work right now.
                   (c)

7. We don't have **much paint** left. There are **much places** we could buy more paint.
                (a)                 (b)

   **Many of** the places are downtown.
     (c)

8. You have **alot of** books. **Many of them** are about colors. Are you **a designer**?
         (a)        (b)                    (c)

**2** Find and correct seven more mistakes in the paragraphs about color forecasting.

**Phil's Picks**

Phil Wilson is ∧*a*color forecaster. He looks at what colors will be popular in much areas like fashion and interior design. Look at the colors he says will become popular.

- Orange is going to be very popular this year in clothing and in the home.

- Much earthy colors, like shades of brown, green, and blue, will be popular in home
5   decorating. However, these earthy colors aren't going to be popular in fashion.

- Wearing much colors at the same time will be fashionable. Wearing alot of colors together is going to be really popular with teenagers.

- Putting unusual colors together is also going to be a trend in fashion – for example, wearing red, orange, and purple together. These colors usually don't go together.

10   Mr. Wilson has been successful at picking alot of color trends in the past. Anna Ramirez, who is interior designer, always considers Phil's advice. She says, "Last year, he said that purple would be popular, and over 50 percent of my clients wanted purple in their homes. This year, I'm going to be ready to use earthy colors and alot of orange!"

# Self-Assessment

Circle the word or phrase that correctly completes each sentence.

1. I painted my room blue, because _____ color blue makes me feel calm.

   a. a     b. the     c. Ø

2. Night Blue is _____ only color of blue paint that the store has.

   a. a     b. the     c. Ø

3. _____ artist usually has a good sense of what colors look good together.

   a. An     b. The     c. Ø

4. Did you know that _____ people can be color blind?

   a. a     b. the     c. Ø

5. Please hand me _____ can of orange paint.

   a. some     b. the     c. Ø

6. _____ interior decorator is someone who designs the inside of a room.

    a. The    b. A    c. An

7. Let's take _____ class. _____ one about the history of color sounds interesting.

    a. a . . . The    b. the . . . A    c. a . . . An

8. _____ research on color blindness was quoted in the student's report.

    a. Not many of    b. Not much    c. Not much of

9. Quite _____ the children said purple was their favorite color.

    a. a few of    b. a few    c. few

10. I know _____ the colors of the rainbow – red, orange, yellow, green, blue, indigo, and violet.

    a. many    b. none of    c. all of

11. Butterflies can see _____ colors. It is crucial for their survival.

    a. a lot    b. a lot of    c. much

12. Gabriel has _____ ability to see the difference between blue and green.

    a. no    b. none    c. not

13. Susan gets a great deal of _____ as a decorator.

    a. works    b. work    c. a work

14. Not many _____ are taking the black and white photography course.

    a. people    b. student    c. woman

15. There isn't any _____ online about the art classes.

    a. materials    b. schedules    c. information

# Pronouns

## Unusual Work Environments

## Reflexive Pronouns

**1** Complete the chart with the correct pronouns.

| Subject Pronoun | Object Pronoun | Reflexive Pronoun |
|---|---|---|
| I | *me* | *myself* |
| you (singular) | | |
| he | | |
| | her | |
| it | | |
| | us | |
| you (plural) | | |
| they | | |

**2** Look at the photos of two types of offices. Complete the sentences with reflexive pronouns.

an open-plan office

an enclosed private office

1. I can't see ___*myself*___ working in an open-plan office because I can only work in calm, quiet places.

2. David imagines _____ working in an open-plan office because he likes to talk to co-workers.

3. Laura, do you tell _____ that you like working in an open-plan office?

4. Fang and Janet enjoy _____ in their open-plan office because they often need to work together and can sit nearby.

5. Sarah likes to talk to _____ , so she prefers working in an enclosed private office.

6. Marc and Sam, can you see _____ working in an open-plan office?

7. An open-plan office _____ can inspire people to be creative.

8. We would have to push _____ to stay focused in an open-plan office because there are more distractions.

**3** Complete the article about a workplace. Use subject, object, and reflexive pronouns.

Imagine _yourself_ working in a creative job with a lot of benefits. Google is one
$\phantom{xx}$(1)

company that has many benefits. Google considers _____ a great place to
$\phantom{xxxxxxxxxxxxxxxxxxxxxxxxxxxxxxxxxxxxxxxxxx}$(2)

work, and others agree. It has made _Fortune_ magazine's "Best 100 Companies to Work For"

in the United States for a number of years.

Google has many benefits for employees and their families. There are onsite fitness

centers for employees' use. The company also has child-care centers in many of its office

sites. Employees can bring their children to work, and _____ can also
$\phantom{xxxxxxxxxxxxxxxxxxxxxxxxxxxxxxxxxxxxxxxxxx}$(3)

bring their pets! However, when employees bring pets with _____ to work,
$\phantom{xxxxxxxxxxxxxxxxxxxxxxxxxxxxxxxxxxxxxxxxxx}$(4)

they have to take care of the pets _____ . There are many cafeterias onsite
$\phantom{xxxxxxxxxxxxxxxxxxxxxxxxxxxxx}$(5)

at Google, and the meals are free. Employees can help _____ to food
$\phantom{xxxxxxxxxxxxxxxxxxxxxxxxxxxxxxxxxxxxxx}$(6)

throughout the day. Employees can also relax in the cafeterias. One Google employee says

that he enjoys _____ during lunch and that many creative ideas come out
$\phantom{xxxxxxxxxxxxxx}$(7)

of casual lunch conversations. One of the company's offices in California even has a car

wash, a dry cleaner's, a beauty salon, and a bike repair shop onsite.

Google employees call _____ "Googlers," and many of
$\phantom{xxxxxxxxxxxxxxxxxxxxxxxxxxxx}$(8)

_____ are happy with their jobs. One of the best things about working for
$\phantom{xx}$(9)

Google is that every Googler's opinion is important. When an employee has an idea, the

company listens to _____ or her.
$\phantom{xxxxxxxxxxxxxxxxx}$(10)

Can you see _____ working at Google?
$\phantom{xxxxxxxxxxxxxx}$(11)

**4** Complete the memo with reflexive pronouns. Add *by* when necessary.

To: All Employees

From: Paula Austin, Vice President

We have had an extremely successful year! I did not accomplish this <u>*by myself*</u> . Every single employee has helped us be successful, and you should all be very proud of _____ .
<br>(1)
<br>(2)

I want to thank a few individual people for their hard work and contributions this year. Sharon Mills started the Sales Reward Program _____ . Without any help, she was able to create a program that will have a great impact on sales and will benefit everyone. Adam Eckhart did the best in the Sales Reward Program. In spite of hurting _____ this year while playing sports and missing a few weeks of work, he still managed to get the most sales. Juan Garcia and Brianna Johnson created a plan to improve employee productivity.[1] The two of them created it _____ - initially without any help from anyone - and then asked for the other employees' comments and suggestions. For every sales goal you reach, you get an hour off. Their idea is working extremely well, and sales have increased even though people are taking more time off. As we enter the next year, you might remind _____ of these examples and contribute your own ideas.
<br>(3)
<br>(4)
<br>(5)
<br>(6)

Our president, Matt Davidson, _____ will be speaking to you next week about our success, but I wanted to tell you the good news _____ before he came. I look forward to the next year being just as successful! Once again, I'd like to thank you for your hard work and creative ideas, and ask you to congratulate _____ for a job very well done.
<br>(7)
<br>(8)
<br>(9)

---
[1]**productivity:** the rate at which a person does useful work

# Pronouns with *Other/Another*

**1** Look at the chart of employee benefits provided by some companies. Complete the sentences with *another*, *others*, *the other*, or *the others* and the correct form of *be*.

| Company | Benefits |
|---------|----------|
| Company A | an on-site doctor, free health care |
| Company B | free counseling,[1] paid tuition,[2] free lunches |
| Company C | free health care, free laundry, free parking, free meals |
| Company D | an on-site gym, flexible hours, free health care |
| Company E | free child care, an on-site doctor, free health care |
| Company F | paid tuition, a company car, a laptop for home use, free lunches |

1. At Company A, one benefit is an on-site doctor. <u>*The other is*</u> free health care.

2. At Company B, one benefit is free counseling. _____ paid tuition.

3. At Company C, one benefit is free health care. _____ free laundry and free parking.

4. At Company D, one benefit is an on-site gym. _____ flexible hours and free health care.

5. At Company E, one benefit is free child care. _____ an on-site doctor and free health care.

6. At Company F, one benefit is paid tuition. _____ a company car and free lunches.

---

[1]**counseling:** professional advice for personal or work problems | [2]**tuition:** money students pay for education

**2** Complete the sentences about some company rules. Use *each other* or *others*.

1. Since there are two people in each office, you should respect <u>*each other*</u> .

2. So that you don't disturb your officemate, speak quietly to _____ when you're on the phone.

3. When you work with a partner on a project, please work cooperatively with _____ .

4. In addition, you'll have weekly meetings with _____ in your group.

5. Please close the conference room door during meetings, so you don't disturb _____ in the office.

**3** Complete the conversation. Use *another*, *each other*, *one another*, or *the other*. Sometimes more than one answer is possible.

**Ms. Smith:** Hello, Morgan. Thank you for coming in. Since this is a new company, I want to get everyone's opinion on how things are going. What have you enjoyed the most about working here?

**Morgan:** I love working with my team – Janice, Paul, and Isabel. At first, I wasn't used to working with a team of people, but I've learned that if we communicate with <u>*each other / one another*</u>, we get a lot done!
(1)

**Ms. Smith:** That's great. Your team works very well together. You obviously respect

_____ . You and Janice seem to work exceptionally well
(2)

with _____ and with _____ teams in the
(3)                                      (4)

office.

**Morgan:** Thanks. Janice and I help _____ a lot. She's good
(5)

at technology, and Paul is good at design, so we all complement

_____ . Of course, it would be great if we could get
(6)

_____ person on our team to help us out when needed.
(7)

**Ms. Smith:** Well, Morgan, I'm very impressed with your work. I look forward to seeing

how your team continues to work with _____ . I'll look into
(8)

getting you _____ team member. Do you have any other
(9)

comments?

**Morgan:** I have two comments. The first is that we could really use _____
(10)

meeting room. _____ meeting rooms we have now are really
(11)

nice, but they're always occupied!

**Ms. Smith:** Yes, we know we need more meeting rooms, but right now we don't have the

money. Maybe in _____ year we can expand. What was
(12)

_____ comment you had?
(13)

**Morgan:** Oh, just that I love working here! Everyone is very nice.

# Indefinite Pronouns

**1 A** Write the indefinite pronouns in the box in the correct columns in the chart.

| ~~anybody~~ | everybody | nobody | somebody |
|---|---|---|---|
| anyone | everyone | no one | someone |
| anything | everything | nothing | something |
| anywhere | everywhere | nowhere | somewhere |

| People | | Places | Things |
|---|---|---|---|
| _anybody_ | _____ | _____ | _____ |
| _____ | _____ | _____ | _____ |
| _____ | _____ | _____ | _____ |
| _____ | _____ | _____ | _____ |

**B** Complete the article about unusual office spaces. Use the indefinite pronouns from A. Sometimes more than one answer is possible.

Google and Facebook both have unusual office spaces. The main office for Google is called the Googleplex. The Googleplex has several cubicles[1] with one side open. People can put almost _anything_ (1) they want in the cubicles, so each cubicle is unique. In one Google office there are many large fish tanks with beautiful fish in them. And there is also a bathtub in front of one of the tanks. _____ (2) in the office can sit there at any time, look at the fish, and relax. In another area, there is an electronic map on one wall. People can see Google locations _____ (3) in the world on the map. There is also a room with a comfortable chair and a bright light. _____ (4) at all can sit in it if he or she needs a break. There is another room with video games in it. There is even a slide at the Googleplex. If you need a break at Google, there is always _____ (5) to do or _____ (6) to relax! _____ (7) working at the Googleplex enjoys the office.

---
[1]**cubicle:** a small divided space in an office

At Facebook, one conference room has a very long table and a long whiteboard all around the room. People can write _____ they (8) need to on the board during meetings. There are no cubicles at Facebook. The offices are open, and _____ works at tables. Some areas (9) have sofas, armchairs, and cushions on the floor so that people can have comfortable meetings. The environment is open, so _____ feels isolated. The office is unique. There is (10) _____ else like it! (11)

In fact, you won't find offices like either of these places _____ else in the (12) world!

**2** Complete the questions with the correct indefinite pronouns. Use the word in parentheses. Then answer the questions with information that is true for you.

1. Do you know _*anyone* OR *anybody*_ (any) who works in an unusual office?

   _____

2. If you could work _____ (any), where would you work?

   _____

3. Does _____ (every) in your family work?

   _____

4. Has a boss ever given you _____ (any) for your birthday?

   _____

5. Have you ever had _____ (no) to say at a meeting?

   _____

# Avoid Common Mistakes

**1** Circle the mistakes.

1. Everyone **gets** to request an office at work. Of course, everybody **want** the window
   (a)                                                              (b)
   office. No one **likes** offices without windows.
   (c)

2. Luiza always gives **herself** enough time to finish projects. Brandon never gives **hisself**
   (a)                                                                        (b)
   enough time. Do you give **yourselves** enough time?
   (c)

3. Everyone **likes** to work with polite co-workers. No one **like** to work in a disorganized
   (a)                                             (b)
   office. Nothing **is** worse than working in an unpleasant environment.
   (c)

4. I have six co-workers in my group. We work well with **one another**. Felipe can be
   (a)
   difficult, but **the others** are easygoing. **Other** in the office wish they worked in my
   (b)                           (c)
   group.

5. Everyone **enjoy** the new employee game room. Someone **is** always using it.
   (a)                                           (b)
   Unfortunately, no one ever **volunteers** to clean it.
   (c)

6. I interviewed for a job along with four **others**. One of the candidates seemed very
   (a)
   nervous, and he didn't seem to believe in **himself**. **The other** looked OK.
   (b)          (c)

7. Natalie wants to give **herself** a raise. The president **himself** told her that she couldn't do
   (a)                                        (b)
   this. Employees can't give **theirselves** raises or promotions.
   (c)

8. The two owners of the company worked with **each other** to give employees great
   (a)
   benefits. Some benefits are good for families, and **others** are good for individuals. Most
   (b)
   of the employees are happy with the benefits, but **other** think they could
   (c)
   be better.

**2** Find and correct eight more mistakes in the paragraphs about unusual work environments.

---

**Unique Work**

Many companies have unusual work environments, but some are more unusual
 *others*
than ~~other~~.

- At Green Mountain Coffee Roasters, employees can go take a class at the onsite
  meditation center. There, they can give theirselves some time to relax, and then
5 go back to work.

- At Chesapeake Energy Corp., employees can take scuba-diving classes. Some
  employees work toward a scuba-diving certification. Other just take the classes
  for fun.

- At Trupanion, a pet health insurance company, everybody receive free pet
10 insurance for their cat or dog.

- A number of companies offer a great benefit: everyone get a free lunch. FactSet
  Research is one company that does this, and other include Google, Facebook,
  and Netflix.

- Camden Property Trust gives a discount to employees who live in the buildings
15 the company owns. Anyone from the company pay 20 percent less in rent.

- Microsoft gives employees free grocery delivery. It also matches donations that
  anyone give to a charity. The founder of the company hisself gives a lot of money
  to charity.

---

# Self-Assessment

Circle the word or phrase that correctly completes each sentence.

1. Do you push _____ hard at work when you have to complete an assignment?

   a. ourselves      b. yourself      c. himself

2. Nick and Ingrid brought their lunch to work with _____ .

   a. them      b. themselves      c. their

3. You don't need to help me. I can do it _____ .

   a. by myself      b. yourself      c. by himself

4. Lenny and Brad, don't be so hard on _____ . You're doing a great job.

   a. youself      b. yourself      c. yourselves

5. The ethnic diversity among employees is one of the two things I like about my office. _____ is the stress-free environment.

   a. Other      b. The other      c. The others

6. I've had five jobs in ten years. One was in an office. _____ was at a school.

   a. Another      b. Other      c. The other

7. I see one of your reports. Where did you put _____ ?

   a. one another      b. another      c. the others

8. The office environment is wonderful because everyone helps _____ .

   a. another      b. the other      c. one another

9. _____ is a better place to work than my office!

   a. No one      b. Nowhere      c. Nothing

10. Aya is _____ who likes to work in an open office.

   a. somebody      b. anybody      c. everybody

11. _____ can work in this office because it's too disorganized.

   a. Everybody      b. Nobody      c. Somebody

12. _____ with a design degree can apply for the job.

   a. Anything      b. Anywhere      c. Anyone

13. Can you trust _____ who works in your office?

   a. everything      b. everyone      c. everywhere

14. There is not another office as special as this one _____ in the world.

   a. nowhere      b. everywhere      c. anywhere

15. _____ in this workspace is modern, including the trendy desks and the lights.

   a. Everything      b. Something      c. Anything

# UNIT 12

## Gerunds

### Getting an Education

## Gerunds as Subjects and Objects

**1** Circle the gerunds in the article. Be careful not to circle the present progressive forms of verbs.

| Elementary School (ages 5–10) | → | Middle School (ages 11–13) | → | High School (ages 14–17) |
|---|---|---|---|---|

(Getting) an education is important to many young people in the United States. In fact, young people must get an education. Starting school at age five, or even younger if they go to preschool, is normal for most students. It depends on the state, but most students don't finish studying until they are 17 or 18. Students go to elementary school, middle school
5  (sometimes called *junior high school*), and then high school.

Many high schools are offering classes that prepare students for college – for example, advanced English, math, and science classes. These classes are called *college prep classes*. However, not attending college is an option. Some students enjoy getting a job right out of school. Taking vocational courses, such as car repair or computer skills, is an option for
10  high school students who are not planning to go to college.

**2** Complete the statements about students' plans. Use the gerund form of the verbs in parentheses.

**John:** I think _working_ (work) after high school is important. I am considering
(1)

_____ (work) at a bank and _____ (move) to L.A.
(2)                                          (3)

**Yawen:** I have two years of high school left, but I've already taken advanced math

classes. _____ (plan) in advance is important, and I'm
(4)

considering _____ (become) an engineer.
(5)

**Sebastian:** I've always imagined _____ (become) a photographer.
(6)

_____ (pay) for the classes is expensive, but my parents have
(7)

been discussing _____ (help) me.
(8)

**90**

**3** Complete the statements with information that is true for you. Use gerunds.

1. I've been discussing _____ with my family.

2. I'm considering _____ next year.

3. When I finish school, I wouldn't mind _____ .

4. I imagine myself _____ in five years.

5. I appreciate not _____ too much.

# Gerunds After Prepositions and Fixed Expressions

**1** Complete the blog entry. Use gerunds with the words in the box.

| about / try | for / learn | ~~in / make~~ | on / use |
|---|---|---|---|
| at / educate | in / apply | of / have | |

### A Solution to My Issues with Education?

Readers of my blog know that I believe _in making_ education available to everyone.
(1)

I dream _____ this happen in my lifetime. I recently heard about a
(2)

new university unlike any other – the University of the People. It started in 2009. The

best part is that it's free! Students are responsible _____ on their own.
(3)

Although students do not have to pay tuition, they do need to plan _____
(4)

a computer and an Internet connection. There are also some fees for the application

and for examinations. Anyone who is interested _____ to the University
(5)

of the People needs to be aware that the university is not accredited.[1] This is not

unusual for a new university, but it's important to know.

Will this educational experiment be successful _____ a large number
(6)

of people? I think it's a good idea, and I hope it's successful. Would you be excited

_____ this approach to education? Please join the online discussion.
(7)

_____
[1]**accredited:** officially approved

**2** Read the conversation. Then answer the questions with gerunds as the objects of prepositions. Use the words in bold from the conversation to help you.

**Nick:** Hi, Ivan. Have you applied to any colleges yet?

**Ivan:** No, I haven't. I'm really worried.

**Nick:** About what?

**Ivan:** I don't know how I'm going to **pay for college**.

5 **Nick:** Well, you should **get financial aid**. You can learn about it from different websites.

**Ivan:** That's a good idea, but I don't like to **do searches on the Internet**. It's hard to find

information.

**Nick:** It's not that hard. I can help you.

**Ivan:** That would be great. I usually **do everything by myself**. What colleges should

10 I apply to?

**Nick:** First, let's concentrate on one thing: how you'll **get money for school**.

**Ivan:** Good idea. I usually **think about too many things at the same time**.

Then I give up.

**Nick:** Well, then I really have to **help you**. I insist! We'll start tomorrow.

15 **Ivan:** Great. Thanks, Nick. I'll **sign up for a computer** at the library.

**Nick:** Good. You take care of that and let me know when to meet you.

1. What is Ivan worried about?

   *He's worried about paying for college.*

2. What does Ivan need to learn about?

   _____

3. What does Ivan complain about?

   _____

4. What is Ivan used to doing?

   _____

5. What does Nick think Ivan should concentrate on?

   _____

6. What does Ivan admit to?

_____

7. What does Nick insist on?

_____

8. What will Ivan take care of?

_____

**3** Complete the sentences with information that is true for you. Use gerunds.

1. I have a good reason for _____ .

2. In class, I have difficulty _____ .

3. I don't have trouble _____ .

4. After class, I spend time _____ .

5. I have an interest in _____ after I finish my
English classes.

# Gerunds After Nouns + *of*

**1** Rewrite the sentences. Replace the words in bold with gerunds and the words in
parentheses.

1. Julia is **currently making** plans for college next year. (in the process of)

   *Julia is in the process of making plans for college next year.*

2. She understands **it is important to go** to college. (the importance of)

   _____

3. She thinks **the price to attend** college is expensive. (the cost of)

   _____

4. Julia is trying to figure out **how to pay** for college. (the best way of)

   _____

5. She's not sure **it's a good idea to take out** a student loan. (about the benefits of)

   _____

6. She is excited **that she may get** a grant. (about the possibility of)

   _____

**2** Complete the paragraphs about student loans. Use the nouns in the box with the gerund form of the verbs in parentheses with *of*.

| advantage | disadvantage | fear | ~~habit~~ | risk | way |
|---|---|---|---|---|---|

You need to be careful when you take out a student loan.

Some students are in the _habit of using_ (use) loan money for
(1)
things like rent and entertainment instead of books and tuition.

This _____ (spend) money
(2)
can lead to problems for students. For example, there is the

_____ (not have) enough
(3)
money for school expenses.

One _____ (borrow) money with a student
(4)
loan is that you usually don't have to pay it back until after you have graduated.

However, a _____ (get) a student loan is
(5)
that once you graduate, you have to start paying back a lot of money. This can be

difficult for students who don't get a job after graduation. However, don't let the

_____ (pay) back a student loan stop you.
(6)
You just need to be careful and be aware of the dangers.

# Avoid Common Mistakes

**1** Circle the mistakes.

1. My sister goes to college full time, and she is also responsible for (**clean**) the house,
(a)
   **cooking** all the meals, and **taking** care of the children.
   (b)                                (c)

2. **Eliminate** all fees for college students who need financial aid **is** one way to help
   (a)                                                              (b)
   students. **Providing** free books is another way.
   (c)

3. Fixing computers **are** something Dan is good at. He plans on **working** for a large
   (a)                                                            (b)
   computer company one day. Finishing his degree **is** his goal right now.
   (c)

4. Our visitors' main interest in **being** here today is not in **seeing** our whole campus.
   (a)                              (b)
   **Visit** our new library is all they're really interested in.
   (c)

5. **Opening** an online university related to **saving** energy **are** sure to attract a lot of
   (a)                                        (b)               (c)
   attention.

6. Many of our international students are concerned about **not be** able to find good
   (a)
   housing. They worry about **finding** an inexpensive place to live or **having** to live too far
   (b)                                                              (c)
   away from campus.

7. Jennifer works on her own in an office at a small university. She spends a lot of time
   **interviewing** all applicants and **filling out** a report on each one. **Have** an assistant
   (a)                              (b)                                    (c)
   would help her a lot.

8. **Scheduling** classes at different times **benefits** students. Many students depend on
   (a)                                       (b)
   **take** classes early in the morning or at night, so they can work during the day.
   (c)

**2** Find and correct nine more mistakes in the paragraph about Pam's studies and career.

---

**Pam's Plans**

       *spending*

After ~~spend~~ two years at a community college, Pam decided that she did not want to

transfer to the four-year university in her city. She thought about become a dog trainer

instead. She had dreamed of be a dog trainer since she was very young. She asked a

friend for advice. Her friend suggested volunteering at the Humane Society. Try to get a

5  job at a pet store to gain experience was another idea. Her friend also suggested reading

books and articles about dog training. After talking to her friend, Pam spent time online

searching for information. Check out websites were another good suggestion from her

friend. Interview veterinarians in the community also seemed like a good idea. Become a

dog trainer began to look more difficult than she had realized. She decided to transfer to

10  the university to study animal science and volunteer at the Humane Society in her spare

time. Concentrating on her studies are making her happy these days. Studying animal

science are the best decision she's ever made!

---

# Self-Assessment

Circle the word or phrase that correctly completes each sentence.

1.  Going to college _____ expensive in many places.

    a. being     b. are     c. is

2.  Jorge imagines _____ a nurse some day.

    a. becoming     b. become     c. became

3.  _____ long hours gives students more time to study.

    a. Not work     b. Not working     c. No working

4.  Michelle _____ to a small college.

    a. is considering going     b. is considering go     c. considering going

5.  Mona and Kelly discussed _____ to the same colleges.

    a. is applying     b. are applying     c. applying

6.  I dislike _____ so much for my books. I don't have any money left for fun!

    a. paying     b. pay     c. am paying

7.  Fixing computers _____ what Mike and Lucinda are good at.

    a. be     b. are     c. is

8.  Are you _____ moving to a new city for school?

    a. afraid in     b. afraid of     c. afraid

9.  Ji Sung learned about _____ financial aid on the Internet.

    a. getting     b. get     c. his getting

10. Mary wasted a lot of money _____ computer games instead of saving it for her books.

    a. buying     b. buy     c. bought

11. Did you have _____ concentrating in the advanced math class?

    a. time     b. money     c. trouble

12. I have a good _____ not finishing my homework.

    a. interest in     b. excuse for     c. in favor of

13. What is the benefit _____ to so many colleges?

    a. of apply      b. of applying      c. applying

14. Mike complained about _____ so many classes in one semester. He has seven classes.

    a. take      b. to take      c. taking

15. I am interested in _____ next year after I graduate. My parents prefer that I go to college.

    a. to work      b. work      c. working

## Infinitives with Verbs

**1** Complete the web article. Use the infinitive form of the verbs in the boxes.

| be | become | increase | not have | not waste | ~~show~~ | teach | work |

### The Kay Morgan Agency, Inc.
*Innovative Ways to Market Your Business*

The Kay Morgan Agency hates it when good companies fail just because they don't market

their products well. We would like _to show_ you how you can advertise your company in
(1)

new and innovative ways. In 2007, we attempted _____ with local
(2)

businesses that needed more creative marketing strategies. In the years since then, we have

offered _____ businesses how to make the best use of marketing
(3)

both here and around the country. We have expanded our business across North America, and

we hope _____ a global company in the future.
(4)

The Kay Morgan Agency works with companies of all sizes. Sometimes large companies

seem _____ conservative in their advertising strategies,
(5)

so we help them be more creative. On the other hand, small business owners tend

_____ the tools they need for advertising. It doesn't matter if
(6)

you're a large or small company. When you hire The Kay Morgan Agency, we'll manage

_____ your sales in two months. Contact us today and find out what
(7)

we can do to help you. We promise _____ your time.
(8)

**2** Complete the article about innovative marketing. Circle the correct form of the verbs. Sometimes more than one answer is possible.

With all of the innovative ways to market products, word-of-mouth can still be a very effective way to advertise. Take Jim Harris as an example. He was starting a painting business. He wanted (**to get**)/ **him to get** as many customers as possible, but he didn't
(1)
have a lot of money for advertising. He offered **to paint / her to paint** the office of a
(2)
veterinarian[1] in his town. Dr. Lee, the veterinarian, agreed. She wanted **to put / him to put**
(3)
pictures of animals on the walls, so he chose **to create / her to create** a large painting
(4)
with various pets, such as cats, dogs, turtles, and birds. It filled an entire wall.

When he was finished painting, Jim asked **to leave / him to leave** some of his business
(5)
cards at the front desk. Leaving his cards helped **to advertise / them to advertise** his
(6)
business. Many people who came into the office commented on the painting, and Dr. Lee asked if they would like **to take / them to take** one of Jim's business cards. Many people
(7)
took one, and some of them asked **to paint / Jim to paint** their homes. Today, Jim has a
(8)
successful business that started by word-of-mouth.

---
[1]**veterinarian:** an animal doctor

**3** Unscramble the sentences. Use the simple past form of one verb and the infinitive form of the other verb.

1. help / the Linden advertising agency / Marcelo Garcia / his clothing business / market

   *The Linden advertising agency helped Marcelo Garcia to market his clothing business.*

2. spend / him / Ms. Linden / more money on advertising / tell

   _____

3. creative advertising methods / urge / him / she / use

   _____

4. her / give / him / ask / he / some ideas

   _____

5. put / choose / Marcelo / ads in teen magazines

   _____

6. young consumers / buy / the advertisements / Marcelo's clothing / persuade

   _____

# Infinitives vs. Gerunds

**1 A** Phone Globe asked customers to complete an online service survey. Write sentences about Nicole's survey answers. Use the underlined verbs with infinitives or gerunds.

We hope our customers at Phone Globe are happy with their cell phones. Please take a few minutes to fill out this survey and help us improve our service.

**Click on the word that best describes how you feel about doing these things on your cell phone:**

|  | Love | Like | Don't like | Hate |
|---|---|---|---|---|
| 1. Sending text messages | ● | ○ | ○ | ○ |
| 2. Calling friends | ○ | ○ | ○ | ● |
| 3. Checking e-mail | ○ | ● | ○ | ○ |
| 4. Using the Internet | ○ | ○ | ● | ○ |

**Click on the choice that you <u>prefer</u>:**

| | |
|---|---|
| 5. Taking pictures with a phone | ○ |
| Taking pictures with a camera | ● |
| 6. Checking e-mail on your phone | ● |
| Checking e-mail on your computer | ○ |

**Click on the answer to the questions:**

|  | Last year | More than a year ago |
|---|---|---|
| 7. When did you <u>begin</u> using our phone service? | ● | ○ |

|  | Yes | No |
|---|---|---|
| 8. Will you <u>continue</u> using our phone service? | ● | ○ |

1. (infinitive)   *Nicole loves to send text messages on her cell phone.*

2. (gerund) _____

3. (infinitive) _____

4. (gerund) _____

5. (infinitive) _____

6. (gerund) _____

7. (infinitive) _____

8. (gerund) _____

**B** Answer the questions with your own opinions. If the question uses a gerund, answer with an infinitive. If the question uses an infinitive, answer with a gerund. Write sentences that are true for you.

1. What do you think about sending text messages?

   _____

2. Do you prefer to call friends or to send them text messages?

   _____

3. Do you like to use the Internet on your phone?

   _____

4. Do you prefer taking pictures with a phone or with a camera?

   _____

5. Do you prefer to check e-mail on your phone or on a computer?

   _____

**3** Complete the paragraph. Circle the correct gerunds or infinitives.

   Last night, Dan stopped **to read /** (**reading**) his marketing homework at 8:00. He wasn't
                                              (1)
finished, but he planned to finish it at lunch today. Unfortunately, he didn't remember

**to put / putting** the article in his book bag last night. At lunch, he realized that he had
       (2)
forgotten **to bring / bringing** the article to school. He remembered **to leave / leaving** it
                   (3)                                                            (4)
on his desk at home. He regretted **not to have / not having** the article with him so that
                                              (5)
he could finish reading it. Before class, he stopped **to discuss / discussing** his problem
                                                                 (6)
with Sally. He tried **to get / getting** her to tell him about the article, but she wouldn't do
                            (7)
it. In fact, she stopped **to discuss / discussing** the problem completely, and she walked
                                   (8)
away. In class, Dan tried **to pretend / pretending** that he had read the article. It worked
                                   (9)
for a few minutes, but when the teacher called on him to answer a question about the end

of the article, he admitted that he hadn't finished it. She replied, "I regret **to tell / telling**
                                                                                       (10)
you that you'll have to stay after class to talk with me about not doing your homework."

# Infinitives After Adjectives and Nouns

**1** Complete the web article with the pairs of phrases and words in the box. Use the infinitive form of the second verb in each pair. Sometimes more than one answer is possible.

| | | |
|---|---|---|
| be easy / do | not be afraid / give away | not be necessary / shock |
| be likely / buy | not be difficult / post | will be amazed / discover |
| be lucky / become | ~~not be embarrassed / let~~ | will be surprised / find |
| be ready / hear | | |

Do you play music in a band? Is your band tired of playing to small audiences?

**Here are some tips on how to advertise your band.**

- _Do not be embarrassed to let_ others hear and see you on their computers.
  (1)

  It _____ a video of your band online.
  (2)

  You _____ how many people go
  (3)

  to see a band after hearing them online. They hear one song, and they

  _____ more.
  (4)

- _____ some music for free. You
  (5)

  _____ that sales often increase when
  (6)

  you give away free music. Let listeners download one song for free, and they

  _____ more songs.
  (7)

- Many artists today think they have to do something dramatic to get people to listen

  to their work, but it _____ your audience to
  (8)

  get attention. It _____ what everyone else
  (9)

  is doing, but you'll be more successful if you do your own thing.

- Remember that bands _____ well known.
  (10)

  Be patient and have fun while you are trying to be successful!

**2** Complete the sentences about Marc's new invention with the words in the box. Use the infinitive form of the verbs. Then check (✓) *Agree* or *Disagree* to say whether or not you agree with the statements.

---

### It's a hat. It's sunglasses!

Never lose your sunglasses again!

Buy the Hat-for-Eyes today for only $10.

The first 100 people to order

get one free!

---

| ability / change | chance / sell | ~~decision / hire~~ | time / buy | way / get |
|---|---|---|---|---|

| | Agree | Disagree |
|---|---|---|
| 1. Marc made the _decision to hire_ a marketing expert. | _____ | _____ |
| 2. His ad is one _____ a lot of attention. | _____ | _____ |
| 3. He'll have the _____ his product to a lot of people. | _____ | _____ |
| 4. His product has the _____ lives. | _____ | _____ |
| 5. It's _____ a Hat-for-Eyes! | _____ | _____ |

---

# Avoid Common Mistakes

**1** Circle the mistakes.

1. Lori **wants to start** a company. She (**wants that people buy**) her product. She really
   (a)                                         (b)
   **needs to get** marketing advice.
   (c)

2. **Jeff forgot to read** the marketing report, so **he decided to not finish** his homework.
   (a)                                              (b)
   **He doesn't seem to care** much about his grades.
   (c)

3. Luisa **loves to seeing** new bands. She **looks forward to listening** to new music online.
   (a)                              (b)
   Sometimes, she **decides to buy** the music.
   (c)

4. It's **easy to market** new products nowadays, but it's **important to find** the best way.
   (a)                                                  (b)
   A very effective **way for advertise** to young customers is on social networking sites.
   (c)

5. Alex **doesn't admit to make** mistakes very often. She **can't stand making** mistakes at
   (a)                                          (b)
   work. She **confessed to making** a mistake with the marketing plan.
   (c)

6. Larry **planned to not buy** a computer for a long time. An advertisement that he saw
      (a)
**persuaded him to get** a new computer. He **promised not to fall** for ads in the future.
      (b)                            (c)

7. I **want to believe** what the company says about this product, but I'm really
      (a)
**worried that it won't work**. I **want that the company give** my money back if it
      (b)                  (c)
doesn't work.

8. I **hope to take** a marketing class next year. I **plan for study** international marketing.
      (a)                             (b)
I **love learning** about ways people market products in other places.
    (c)

**2** Find and correct the mistakes in the article about false advertising.

---

**False Advertising**

    False advertising is giving untrue information about a product. Some stores use false advertising because they want ~~that~~ you ^*to* come inside. Here are some common forms of false advertising that stores use to persuade you to buying their products:

- Some companies use pictures that make their products look better than they are.
5    Maybe you see a picture of a great computer online. When you get to the store, the computer looks very different. The salespeople then offer you another, more expensive, computer.

- Some stores advertise great sales. You look forward to buy the product you see, but when you get to the store, the item you want for buy is gone. Once you're in the store,
10    salespeople urge you to not leave without buying something.

- Some advertisements or salespeople say a product can do something that it can't do. They convince that you get it, and then you're disappointed when you get home.
    Be careful of false advertising when you shop. We don't want that you be disappointed.

---

# Self-Assessment

Circle the word or phrase that correctly completes each sentence.

1. The company's advertisements tend _____ incorrect.

   a. be     b. to be     c. being

2. I hope _____ my marketing homework before midnight.

   a. finish     b. to finish     c. finishing

3. The marketing director promised _____ anyone with the new ads.

   a. to not shock     b. not to shocking     c. not to shock

4. Did you want to buy a new computer, or did the salesperson convince _____ ?

   a. you get it     b. to get it     c. you to get it

5. I chose _____ a new cell phone. The ad made it look great!

   a. to buy     b. it to buy     c. me to buy

6. Did you ask _____ the report today? I don't think he's done yet.

   a. to finish     b. Dustin to finish     c. Dustin finishing

7. The company began _____ a lot of sales after it advertised online.

   a. to get     b. get     c. to getting

8. Paul can't stand _____ advertisements in his e-mail.

   a. receive     b. receiving     c. to not receive

9. We stopped _____ our product because it wasn't good for the environment.

   a. to sell     b. selling     c. sell

10. Don't forget _____ at products carefully before you buy them. Sometimes companies use false advertising.

   a. to look     b. looking     c. look

11. I tried _____ into the marketing class, but I wasn't able to.

   a. to get     b. getting     c. to getting

12. Jen is afraid _____ the international marketing class because her brother said it was difficult.

   a. take     b. to take     c. taking

13. It's easy _____ which marketing strategies work the best.

   a. to see     b. to seeing     c. for see

14. Don has the ability _____ ads for social networking sites.

   a. to create     b. creating     c. creates

15. I had _____ a salesperson, but I didn't want to do it.

   a. a chance being     b. a chance to be     c. a chance I am

# UNIT 14

## Negative Questions and Tag Questions

### Geographic Mobility

## Negative Questions

**1** Complete the conversation with the negative question forms of the verbs in parentheses. Read the answers to the questions to help you with the verb forms.

**Dan:** Hey, Ben. What are you doing?

**Ben:** I'm reading research on geographic mobility in 2010. It's for my government class.

**Dan:** Oh . . . I read a few articles about this last semester. _Didn't_ a lot of people in the
(1)
United States _move_ (move) in 2010?
(1)

**Ben:** No, not really. Only 12.5 percent of the people in the United States moved.

**Dan:** Interesting. In general, _____ a lot of people _____
(2)                                              (2)
(move) to better homes?

**Ben:** Yes, almost half of the people who moved in 2010 did it for housing reasons.

**Dan:** What about other reasons? _____ people also _____
(3)                                              (3)
(change) cities in 2010 because of jobs?

**Ben:** Yes. A little more than 16 percent of the people who moved did so for work.

**Dan:** OK, but _____ (be) there other reasons for moving, too?
(4)

**Ben:** Yes, there are. People often move because of changes in their family situations.

**Dan:** I heard that people don't usually move far. _____ people often
(5)
_____ (stay) in the same area when they move?
(5)

**Ben:** Sure. In 2010, about 82 percent of the people who moved stayed in the same state.

**Dan:** Are the statistics only about people who moved within the United States?

_____ they _____ (include) people who moved to the
(6)                              (6)
United States from other countries in 2010?

**Ben:** Of course they do. In total, about 3.5 percent of the people who moved came to the
United States from foreign countries.

**2** Mr. Evans, a school principal, is speaking with Sofia on the phone about a teaching job. He doesn't have her résumé with him and can't remember all the information in it. Write negative questions with the words in parentheses. Then complete Sofia's answers with the information in her résumé.

> **Sofia Alba**
>
> **Work**
>
> 2008–Present   Dylan High School   Chicago, Illinois
> *English Teacher*
>
> 2006–2008   North American School   Mexico City, Mexico
> *English Teacher*
>
> **Education**
>
> 2005   Martinson College   New York, New York
> *B.A., Education*
>
> **Other Languages**
>
> Spanish and French

1. (graduate / from Martinson College)

   **Mr. Evans:** *Didn't you graduate from Martinson College?*

   **Sofia:** *Yes* , that's right. I graduated in _2005_ .

2. (have / a degree in economics)

   **Mr. Evans:** _____

   **Sofia:** _____ . Actually, I have a degree in _____ .

3. (work / at Dyett High School now)

   **Mr. Evans:** _____

   **Sofia:** Actually, _____ . I work at _____ .

4. (live / in Chicago since 2006)

   **Mr. Evans:** _____

   **Sofia:** _____ . Actually, I've lived here since _____ .

5. (move / to Mexico City)

   **Mr. Evans:** _____

   **Sofia:** _____ , that's right. I moved there in _____ .

6. (speak / Spanish and Portuguese)

   **Mr. Evans:** _____

   **Sofia:** Well, actually, I speak _____ .

# Tag Questions

**1** Complete the questions. Circle the correct tags.

1. In the past, large companies were in big cities, **are they / aren't they / were they / (weren't they)**?

2. Now, some companies are moving to smaller cities, **are they / aren't they / is it / isn't it**?

3. It can be cheaper to run a big company in a small city, **is it / isn't it / can it / can't it**?

4. That's not always true, **is it / isn't it / is that / isn't that**?

5. Everybody relocates when a company moves, **do they / don't they / does it / doesn't it**?

6. The owners of our company are deciding whether or not to move our company to a smaller town, **are they / aren't they / do they / don't they**?

7. Our boss hasn't told us the decision yet, **did he / didn't he / has he / hasn't he**?

8. There hasn't been a memo about it, **is there / isn't there / has there / hasn't there**?

9. Some employees won't be happy, **are we / aren't we / will they / do they**?

10. You wouldn't like to relocate, **did it / didn't it / would you / wouldn't you**?

**2** Read the article from an alumni magazine. Complete the statements and tag questions. Then write the answers using the information in the article. Write the correct information after the *No* answers. Sometimes more than one answer is possible.

## The Class of 2011
*What are they doing now?*

Here are the people from the Class of 2011 who have made the biggest changes:

1. Rajat Singh is working at a hospital in Dallas.

2. Jorge and Marta Baeza moved to Miami to start a family.

3. Brandon Harris is painting houses for his brother's company.

4. Olga Galdin moved to London to look for work.

5. Ali and Chuck Trenton bought a restaurant near the college.

6. Isabela Fuentes is living in Houston and teaching English.

1. **A:** Rajat _is working_ at a school, _isn't he_ ?

    **B:** _No, he isn't. He's working at a hospital._

2. **A:** Jorge and Marta _____ to Miami, _____ ?

    **B:** _____

3. **A:** Brandon _____ cars, _____ ?

    **B:** _____

4. **A:** Olga _____ to Lima, _____ ?

    **B:** _____

5. **A:** Ali and Chuck _____ a clothing store, _____ ?

    **B:** _____

6. **A:** Isabela _____ in Houston, _____ ?

    **B:** _____

**3** Read the questions. Then circle the statements that describe what the speaker thinks. Use the intonation arrows to help you.

1. Jen and Marc are living in Alaska, aren't they?

    a. The speaker is not certain this statement is true.

    b. The speaker expects the listener to agree.

2. They moved there to find jobs, didn't they?

    a. The speaker is not certain this statement is true.

    b. The speaker expects the listener to agree.

3. Jen loves cold weather, doesn't she?

    a. The speaker is not certain this statement is true.

    b. The speaker expects the listener to agree.

4. But Marc doesn't like the cold, does he?

    a. The speaker is not certain this statement is true.

    b. The speaker expects the listener to agree.

5. They aren't coming home for the holidays, are they?

    a. The speaker is not certain this statement is true.

    b. The speaker expects the listener to agree.

**4 A** Complete the excerpts from the conversation with *Yes* or *No* short answers.

1. **Jake:** You saw the movie *Winged Migration*, didn't you?

   **Diego:** <u>Yes, I did</u> . It was great.

2. **Jake:** It's about birds migrating, isn't it?

   **Diego:** _____ . It shows

   them moving because of weather.

3. **Jake:** They didn't film it in one year, did they?

   **Diego:** _____ . It took over four years.

4. **Jake:** They filmed some of it in the United States, didn't they?

   **Diego:** _____ . However, they also filmed scenes in

   Iceland, Japan, and other countries.

5. **Jake:** It's available on DVD now, isn't it?

   **Diego:** _____ . Why don't you get it from the library?

**B** Look at the intonation arrows in the conversation in A. For each of Jake's questions, write *U* if he is uncertain of the information or *A* if he expects agreement from Diego.

1. <u>  U  </u>    2. _____    3. _____    4. _____    5. _____

**5** Answer the questions with your own opinion. Use *yes* or *no*, and add one sentence with more information.

1. You would move for a job, wouldn't you?

   _____

2. You didn't move last year, did you?

   _____

3. You won't study another foreign language, will you?

   _____

4. You don't like cold weather, do you?

   _____

5. You enjoy your studies, don't you?

   _____

# Avoid Common Mistakes

**1** Circle the mistakes.

1. Vivian moved to Japan, **didn't she**? You're visiting her next month, **no**? You're going
   <u>(a)</u>          (b)

   with your sister, **aren't you**?
           (c)

2. **A: Isn't the company moving** the main office to a different location soon?
        (a)

       **Aren't the managers supposed to tell** us 60 days before the move?
            (b)

   **B:** Yes, they are. **You no get** the e-mail about it last week?
               (c)

3. **A: Didn't you** hear that Tom got a new job?
        (a)

   **B: No, I didn't**. I'm glad you told me. I guess his income will be higher now, **isn't he**?
       (b)                                           (c)

4. **A:** He'll make a lot more money, and he'll also have to travel a lot. **Isn't it** great?
                                                          (a)

       **Wouldn't you** like to have a job like his?
           (b)

   **B: No**. I'd love to travel for work.
       (c)

5. Julia's making a movie about why people move, **doesn't she**? It's for her film class,
                                            (a)

   **isn't it**? You'll go see it, **won't you**?
     (b)               (c)

6. You can help me, **no**? You're moving to Toronto, **aren't you**? You can take this package
                   (a)                        (b)

   to my brother, **can't you**?
           (c)

7. **A: Aren't you** working from home now?
        (a)

   **B: Yes**. My apartment is too small, so I still go to the office every day. **Don't you** agree
       (b)                                                      (c)

   it's better not to work at home?

8. **A: Isn't Zack helping** his parents move? **They no moving** to Florida?
        (a)                                    (b)

   **B: Yes**, they are, but I don't think Zack is helping them. I think he's on vacation in Hawaii
       (c)

   right now.

**2** Find and correct eight more mistakes in the interview with a doctor who works at a mobile health clinic.[1]

---

**A Moving Doctor**

*Dr. Morris works for a mobile health clinic in Kenya. We interviewed him last week.*

Q: You travel from place to place in Kenya, ~~doesn't he~~ *don't you*?

A: No. I travel a lot. I move from place to place with other doctors and nurses.

Q: You no working mostly in small towns?

5 A: Yes, I am. There aren't many hospitals there. We have a small hospital in a van.

Q: You drive the van from place to place, no?

A: Well, I don't drive it myself. Someone else drives it. We usually stay in a place for

a few weeks. Then we go to another town.

Q: This medical program helps a lot of people, doesn't she?

10 A: Yes, it does. We give health care to many people in small towns.

Q: You no get tired of moving around so much?

A: Yes. I never get tired. I love it.

Q: New doctors will be coming to your program next week, no?

A: Yes, they will. I'm going to be training six new doctors.

15 Q: Then you're going home, isn't it?

A: No, I'm not. Actually, I'm going to Ethiopia to set up a mobile clinic there.

---

[1]**mobile health clinic:** a doctor's office, usually in a van, that travels from place to place

---

# Self-Assessment

Circle the word or phrase that correctly completes each sentence.

1. _____ you work for a moving company?

   a. Not do      b. Do not      c. Don't

2. Was Danilo _____ living in Seoul last year?

   a. not      b. no      c. wasn't

3.  I'm so upset that I didn't get that job! _____ the best person to work in our office in Brazil?

    a. I'm not       b. Am not I       c. Aren't I

4.  Hey, that woman looks like Liz. Didn't she _____ overseas?

    a. move       b. moved       c. not

5.  **A:** Hasn't Yolanda moved to Florida? **B:** _____ . She moved to Miami, in southern Florida.

    a. No.       b. Yes, she has       c. No, she hasn't

6.  They moved to a big city, _____ ?

    a. don't they       b. did they       c. didn't they

7.  You're not from Argentina, _____ ?

    a. aren't you       b. are you       c. do you

8.  You haven't lived in Asia, _____ ?

    a. did you       b. haven't you       c. have you

9.  They were packing boxes, _____ ?

    a. weren't they       b. were they       c. didn't they

10. The students are studying migration trends, _____ ?

    a. aren't we       b. isn't it       c. aren't they

11. _____ a great place to live, isn't it?

    a. That's       b. Something's       c. Everyone's

12. Everyone has some issues with moving, _____ ?

    a. doesn't he       b. doesn't it       c. don't they

13. **A:** Tom moved when he got married, didn't he? **B:** _____ .

    a. Yes, he didn't       b. Yes, he did       c. No, he did

14. **A:** Your neighbors didn't move to New York City, did they? **B:** _____ . They moved to L.A.

    a. No, they didn't       b. Yes, they didn't       c. No, they did

15. **A:** You aren't driving to Seattle, are you? **B:** _____ . I can't afford to fly.

    a. Yes, I have to       b. No, I'm not       c. No, I don't

## *That* Clauses

**1** Add *that* to five more noun clauses in the article.

### Jobs with Values

Many jobs have different values associated with them. Here are just a few:

**Doctors:** Doctors value each patient's life. They even take an oath.[1] The oath
says ∧ doctors must treat sick people to the best of their ability.
    *that*

Doctors also promise to keep a patient's information private.

5 **Lawyers:** Privacy is also important in law. Lawyers know they cannot share a

client's information with others if the client doesn't want them to.

Lawyers also value fairness.

**Teachers:** Teachers value learning. They believe all students can learn.

**Dentists:** Dentists value good dental care. They know their patients will have

10 healthier teeth if they brush and floss them every day and see a

dentist regularly.

**Librarians:** Librarians value reading. They also think people should be quiet in

libraries to let other people concentrate on what they are reading.

**Journalists:** Journalists care about the truth. They learn they must be correct and

15 fair when reporting.

[1]**oath:** an official promise that you will do something

**2** Read the sentences about how different cultures value time. Then rewrite each pair of sentences in bold as a single sentence with a noun clause. Omit *that* for the informal sentences.

1. Dr. Kim is an anthropologist. **He discovered something early in his career: People from different cultures value time differently.**

   *Dr. Kim discovered that people from different cultures value time differently.*
   (formal)

2. Paul is going to study in Brazil. **He assumes something: Brazilians don't usually mind being late for parties with close friends.**

   _____
   (informal)

3. Mr. Ito is researching German culture. **He has read something: Germans usually like to be on time.**

   _____
   (formal)

4. Melissa is visiting a friend in the United States. **She feels something: Americans are sometimes too worried about time.**

   _____
   (informal)

5. Ms. Piper is researching Canadian work habits. **She has noticed something: Canadians usually start meetings on time.**

   _____
   (formal)

6. Carolina is on vacation in Italy. **She has realized something: Sometimes it's not important to be on time in Italy.**

   _____
   (informal)

7. Dr. Robins is an architect, working on a project in China. **He understands something: Chinese people often plan things years in advance.**

   _____
   (formal)

8. Ben is staying in Tokyo. A Japanese friend invited him to a party. **He guesses something: People aren't often late for parties in Japan.**

   _____
   (informal)

**3** Complete the sentences about time. Use *that* clauses. Write sentences that are true for you.

1. I think _that it's important to be on time for dinner at a friend's house_ .
(dinner at a friend's house)

2. I've learned _____ .
(business meetings)

3. I've decided _____ .
(English class)

4. I understand _____ .
(a flight)

5. I believe _____ .
(birthday parties)

# Agreement Between *That* Clauses and Main Clauses

**1** Unscramble the sentences. Use the simple present form of the verbs in the main clause. Put the verbs in the *that* clause in the present, future, or past, as indicated in parentheses. Sometimes more than one answer is possible.

1. respect / say / experts / a common value in most cultures / that / be / (present)

    _Experts say that respect is a common value in most cultures._

2. that / their parents / show / respect / research / most people / (present)

    _____

3. most parents / that / imagine / them / always respect / their children / (future)

    _____

4. deserve / learn / that / most children / grandparents / respect / (present)

    _____

5. people / feel / some historians / show others / that / more respect in the past / (past)

    _____

6. children / think / some teachers / that / be / more respectful in the past / (past)

    _____

7. students / some teachers / that / assume / listen better in the future / (future)

    _____

8. trends / experts / that / realize / change / over time / (future)

    _____

**2** Complete the blog entry. Circle the correct form of the verbs. Use the information in parentheses and the explanations in the box to help you.

---

*after* = The event in the *that* clause happened after the event in the main clause.

*before* = The event in the *that* clause happened before the event in the main clause.

*same* = The event in the *that* clause happened at the same time as the event in the main clause.

*truth* = The *that* clause expresses a universal truth or fact that applies to the present.

---

I traveled a lot for work last year. I discovered that people **had valued /** (**value**)

(1. truth)

personal space differently in different parts of the world. For example, because

I'm Canadian, I know that Canadians **had stood / stand** about three feet apart

(2. truth)

when they talk. After a party at work in Quebec, however, I realized that

people there **had been standing / were going to stand** very close together.

(3. before)

I asked someone I work with about what I had noticed, and I found out that

French-speaking Canadians usually **had liked / like** to stand much closer

(4. truth)

than English-speaking Canadians.

Before I went to Japan, I had looked at some pictures of Tokyo online. I

noticed that people **are / were** generally close together on the streets and in

(5. same)

the subway, so I guessed that I **saw / would see** people very close together

(6. after)

everywhere in Japan. When I was there, though, I realized that people

**didn't stand / doesn't stand** close together at meetings and social events. I

(7. same)

found out that they **are / had been** usually close together on subways and in the

(8. truth)

streets because it is crowded in those places.

I hope that I won't be traveling as much next year. I want my own personal

space and would like to just stay home for a while. Nonetheless, I've learned

something about different cultures and personal space this year.

# *That* Clauses After Adjectives and Nouns

**1** Read the online comments about learning languages. Underline each adjective before a *that* clause. Circle each noun before a *that* clause.

> Different cultures have different views on learning languages. What do you think about learning languages?
>
> **JL22:** People in the United States often know only one language, but it's <u>clear</u> that people in Europe usually learn more than one language.
>
> 5  **KyleK:** It's <u>understandable</u> that Europeans know many languages. The countries are close together, and they need to communicate with each other.
>
> **DougT:** It's <u>unfortunate</u> that people in the United States don't speak more languages. It's my (view) that there are many benefits to being bilingual![1]
>
> 10  **Mary96:** It is <u>evident</u> that bilingual people have advantages. It's <u>understandable</u> that bilingual people get better jobs.
>
> **Sandra:** The (problem) is that not many schools in the United States offer enough foreign language classes.
>
> **George06:** I disagree. My (impression) is that schools offer classes, but it's very challenging to find places to speak other languages outside of class.
>
> 15
>
> **JavierR:** I'm <u>certain</u> that people in my country value language learning. Almost everyone learns Spanish and English in school.
>
> **L1990:** My (hope) is that everyone will speak both Spanish and English in the next 20 years.
>
> 20  **Mei92:** My (concern) is that people will still only be bilingual. It's <u>fortunate</u> that we speak three languages in my family.
>
> **Isabel:** In some places there's a (belief) that learning only one language is the best. I guess the (point) is that a lot of us disagree!
>
> ---
> [1]**bilingual:** able to speak two languages

**2** Write sentences with *that* clauses. Use *It is* or *The . . . is* in the main clauses.

1. understandable / different cultures have different values

   *It is understandable that different cultures have different values.*

2. clear / different cultural values should be respected

   _____

3. problem / something considered positive by one culture might be considered negative by another

   _____

4. interesting / the Internet might help reduce these problems by making people more aware of other cultures

   _____

5. hope / people will learn more about cultural values in other countries

   _____

6. likely / there will be fewer conflicts because of different cultural values in the future

   _____

**3** Complete the sentences with *that* clauses. Use the topics in the box or your own ideas. Write sentences that are true for you.

| family life | personal relationships | speaking two languages | work |
| money | privacy | traditions | values |

1. I think it's surprising _____ .

2. I am certain _____ .

3. I have the impression _____ .

4. My concern is _____ .

5. It is my belief _____ .

6. I find it unfortunate _____ .

7. I think it's interesting _____ .

# Avoid Common Mistakes

**1** Circle the mistakes.

1. (John recognized, that) cultural values were different in Mexico than they were in his
   <br>(a)
   country. **He realized that** people viewed time differently. He found out **he was** able to
   <br>(b) <br>(c)
   adapt easily.

2. It's disappointing **that Chinese classes aren't** available at our school. I'm not sure
   <br>(a)
   **that people value** learning other languages enough. I hope **that more language classes be**
   <br>(b) <br>(c)
   available in the future.

3. It's embarrassing **that don't speak Spanish better**. I realize **that it's important** to speak
   <br>(a) <br>(b)
   other languages. It's true **that I've been trying**, but it's difficult for me.
   <br>(c)

4. **Research shows that** values differ in different cultures. **Experts do not believe, that**
   <br>(a) <br>(b)
   one culture is right and another is wrong. **They think that** it is important to understand
   <br>(c)
   the differences.

5. Diana and Jim realize **that they should respect** their parents. Their parents are relieved
   <br>(a)
   **that their children understand** this value as well. They feel lucky **that have** respectful
   <br>(b) <br>(c)
   children.

6. Tom **understands that culture** influences **values, but** he's **not sure, that his values**
   <br>(a) <br>(b) <br>(c)
   are influenced by culture.

7. Many cultures believe **that hard work is** important. Research shows **that this idea is**
   <br>(a) <br>(b)
   usually true in these cultures – people who work harder are usually more successful and
   happier. According to psychologists, it is not surprising **that parents teaching** their
   <br>(c)
   children this value.

8. I'm glad **that I'm learning** about different cultures. I'm surprised **that I learning** so
   <br>(a) <br>(b)
   much in this class. I'm disappointed **that the class is going to end** soon.
   <br>(c)

**2** Find and correct seven more mistakes in the article about diverse cities.

---

**Diverse Cities in the World**

There are many places in the world that are culturally diverse. It is interesting ^*that* people with different cultural values can often get along well in these places. Here are some of the most diverse cities in the world.

**New York City:** It is clear that New York City always been culturally diverse. People
5  speak around 800 languages in the city. Immigrants have come to New York City from all over the world, and experts are certain that the trend continue in the future.

**Toronto:**  Toronto is Canada's most diverse city. It is true, that French and English are official languages in Canada, but research shows that almost one-third of the people in Toronto speak a foreign language at home. Over half of the people living in Toronto were
10  not born in Canada.

**Los Angeles:** Los Angeles is another diverse city. Research shows, that almost half of the population is Latino, 14 percent is Asian, and 9 percent is African American. L.A. is diverse in other ways, too. Experts say that is the creative capital of the world.

**London:** One website says that, almost every culture in the world can be found in
15  London. The large number of cultures is reflected in the restaurants, in which you can find a variety of food from around the world.

**Dubai:** Dubai is quickly becoming a diverse city. It is surprising that was not diverse in the past. Many people from around the world have moved there for work, making it a global city today.

---

# Self-Assessment

Circle the word or phrase that correctly completes each sentence.

1. This book says _____ affects the way we think.

   a. that       b. that culture       c. is

2. Briana _____ all journalists should tell the truth.

   a. believes, that       b. believes that,       c. believes that

3. Doctors take an oath that says they _____ all patients to the best of their ability.

   a. treated       b. will treat       c. have treated

4. Do you _____ that people have different values?

   a. understand       b. show       c. have

5. Many Americans feel that individualism _____ extremely important today.

   a. not be       b. is       c. was

6. Historians recognize that people _____ hard to survive in the past.

   a. work       b. are working       c. worked

7. I have decided that I _____ Japanese next year.

   a. will study       b. study       c. have studied

8. My parents knew that I _____ respectful to my teachers at the meeting yesterday.

   a. was       b. am       c. will be

9. The study showed that most teenagers _____ their grandparents.

   a. are going to respect       b. respect       c. will respect

10. Ms. Lang found out that her students _____ the homework on values. They had to do it together in class.

    a. aren't completing       b. hadn't completed       c. won't complete

11. I heard that Dr. Roberts _____ his books at the new bookstore.

    a. selling       b. would selling       c. would be selling

12. It's _____ that I won't understand the culture in a country whose language I don't speak.

    a. likely       b. unlikely       c. fortunate

13. _____ clear that Erica loves to learn about other cultures.

    a. It's     b. It     c. She

14. It was our _____ that Rich wouldn't move to another country.

    a. possibility     b. difference     c. impression

15. The _____ is that no one understands us.

    a. problem     b. views     c. frightening

# Noun Clauses with *Wh-* Words and *If/Whether*

## Inventions They Said Would Never Work

## Noun Clauses with *Wh-* Words

**1** Complete the excerpts from a conversation about Thomas Edison. Use *how, how many, what, when, where, which, who,* or *why*.

1. **A:** I can't remember <u>*when*</u> Thomas Edison was born.

   **B:** He was born in 1847.

2. **A:** I don't know _____ Edison was born.

   **B:** He was born in Ohio in the United States.

3. **A:** I wonder _____ brothers and sisters Edison had.

   **B:** He had six brothers and sisters.

   **A:** Do you know _____ was the youngest?

   **B:** He was!

4. **A:** I wonder _____ Edison became interested in science.

   **B:** I know he was just a child. Edison always wanted to figure out _____ things worked.

5. **A:** I'd like to know _____ Edison didn't talk until he was four years old. What was the reason?

   **B:** I don't know, but I do know this . . . when he started to talk, he was always asking questions!

6. **A:** I'd like to know _____ new things Thomas Edison invented.

   **B:** I don't know for sure, but he had over 1,000 patents.

7. **A:** I know _____ invention was Edison's most famous!

   **B:** I know that one, too – the light bulb!

8. **A:** Did you know that Thomas Edison had substantial hearing loss by age 12?

   **B:** I don't know _____ caused his hearing loss.

   **A:** Experts have different opinions on the cause. Regardless, Edison became one of the most important inventors in U.S. history.

**2** Complete the article with *how*, *what*, *when*, or *where* and the words in parentheses. Use the simple present or infinitive form of the verbs. Sometimes more than one answer is possible.

<u>*What is*</u> (be) amazing about online shopping is that in 1966, *Time* magazine said it
(1)
would never work! Most people today are comfortable with online shopping, but there are

some things you should consider when you buy items online.

- You have to understand _____ (expect) as extra costs. Most
(2)
companies charge money for shipping.[1] Depending on _____
(3)
(the item / come) from and _____ (you / want) it, this can get
(4)
expensive.

- It's important to remember that _____ (you / see)
(5)
isn't always _____ (you / get). You need to learn
(6)
_____ (look) for important details in the photographs and descriptions
(7)
of products. Even when you do this, there are sometimes surprises when the item arrives.

- Finally, it's a good idea to know _____ (find) reviews of products.
(8)
It can be very helpful to see _____ (people / say) about products.
(9)

[1]**shipping:** the act of sending something to a customer

**3** Unscramble the sentences about an alternative fuel.

1. are trying / how / algae[1] into fuel / to turn / researchers / to figure out

    <u>*Researchers are trying to figure out how to turn algae into fuel.*</u>

2. can be used in cars / they / when / the "algae fuel" / still don't know

    _____

3. with the research / what / happens / many people / care about

    _____

4. may affect / of the project / the results / we power our cars in the future / how

    _____

5. will happen / I'm / not sure / what / with this new technology

    _____

6. however, I / why / can understand / are interested in it / so many people

    _____

[1]**alga:** (plural *algae*) a type of plant that grows in water

# Noun Clauses with *If / Whether*

**1** Complete the conversation. Use the questions in the box to complete the noun clauses with *if / whether*.

> Is Sandwich the name of a place?
> Did it happen in the 17th or 18th century?
> Did the earl like his sandwich?
> Did the sandwich become popular right away?
> ~~Did you read the article on the naming of the sandwich?~~
> Is the place in England or North America?
> Was the name from the servant who prepared it or from the man who ate it?

**Ms. Moore:** OK, class. Let's talk about the homework. I'd like to know whether or not

_you read the article on the naming of the sandwich_.
(1)

Dan, where did the sandwich get its name?

**Dan:** Well, I don't remember whether _____
(2)
_____.

**Yuko:** I remember! It was from the man who ate it. The story is that the fourth Earl of

Sandwich was playing a card game, and he wanted to eat while he played. His

servant put some meat between two pieces of bread so that the Earl could eat

quickly and not stop playing. So the sandwich got its name from the man

who ate it!

**Ms. Moore:** Yes, that's right, Yuko. When did it happen?

**Yuko:** I forgot if _____.
(3)

**Dan:** I know that! It happened in the 18th century. I wonder whether or not

_____.
(4)

**Mike:** He did! He really liked it and thought it was a great idea! But I can't remember if

_____.
(5)

**Yuko:** Yes, it is the name of a place, but for some reason I can't remember whether

_____.
(6)

**Dan:** It's in England. I wonder if _____.
(7)

**Mike:** I don't know, but it's very popular nowadays, right?

**2** Read the headline from an article about a new refrigerator. Then rewrite the sentences by replacing _whether_ with _if_. When _if_ is not possible, write **✗**. Change the positions of _or not_ when necessary.

---

## Scientists Work on Low-energy Refrigerator Based on 1930 Einstein Patent
### Full article on page 6

---

1. I don't know whether or not Einstein's refrigerator worked.

   _I don't know if Einstein's refrigerator worked or not._

2. Einstein probably thought about whether he'd make money from his creation.

   _✗_

3. He certainly cared about whether the refrigerator would be good for the environment or not.

   _____

4. Some people couldn't figure out whether or not Einstein's invention was practical.

   _____

5. I'd like to find out whether today's version is practical.

   _____

6. The researchers had to decide whether to share the information with the public.

   _____

7. I don't know whether or not today's version will have financial success.

   _____

**3** Rewrite the sentences about the invention contest finalists. Use the words in parentheses and _or_.

1. **Rafael:** I don't know which one will win.

   _I don't know if the Ring Phone or the_

   _Scooter Shoes will win._
   (if)

2. **Betsy:** I don't care which one will make more money.

   _____

   _____
   (whether)

3. **Ted:** They're trying to decide which one will get first prize.

_____
(if)

4. **Mia:** I don't remember which one my cousin invented.

_____
(whether)

5. **Lori:** I'm trying to find out which one will get a patent first.

_____
(if)

6. **Ahmet:** I can't figure out which one will be more practical.

_____
(whether)

# Noun Clauses in Direct and Indirect Questions

**1** Rewrite the questions about an invention: "hair" that comes in a can. Use the words in parentheses and the correct punctuation.

1. What are the world's worst inventions? (Do you know)

   _Do you know what the world's worst_
   _inventions are?_

2. Who invented hair that comes in a can? (I was wondering)

   _____

   _____

3. How does the product work? (Can you explain)

   _____

4. Why would someone want to put colored powder on his or her head? (I'd like to know)

   _____

5. Does anyone buy this product? (I want to find out / if)

   _____

6. Does the product really look like hair? (Can anyone tell me / whether)

   _____

**2** Rewrite each question as a direct or indirect question. Sometimes more than one answer is possible.

1. Do men or women use hair that comes in a can? (direct question)

   *Do you know whether men or women use hair that comes in a can?* OR

   *Can anyone tell me if men or women use hair that comes in a can?*

2. Can you use it on animals? (indirect question)

   _____

3. What colors does it come in? (direct question)

   _____

4. How much does it cost? (indirect question)

   _____

5. Can you buy it in stores or online? (direct question)

   _____

# Avoid Common Mistakes

**1** Circle the mistakes.

1. I don't know **if Tom's umbrella is for the rain or snow**. He has tested different
   (a)
   materials, but he's having trouble deciding (**either he'll make it with plastic or nylon**).
   (b)
   Do you have any idea **whether or not you'd use it**?
   (c)

2. I don't know **what my friend is inventing**. I doubt **if his invention will be successful**.
   (a)                                                        (b)
   I wonder **when will he finish**.
   (c)

3. The company wants to know **if anyone would buy their product**. They also want to
   (a)
   find out **wether it would be more popular with teenagers or adults**. They need to
   (b)
   know **whether or not it's easy to use**.
   (c)

4. John has to decide **either or not to return his cell phone**. I sometimes really wonder
   (a)
   **if the company knows what a terrible product the phone is**. But that's not
   (b)
   important. What is important is **whether they will give John his money back or not**.
   (c)

5. Do you know **wether or not Julie fixed her invention**? I heard from some friends
   (a)
   **that it doesn't work well in bad weather**. Do you know **if it works when the weather is good**?
   (b)                                                          (c)

6. Can you help me with my invention? I need to figure out **either or not it's a good idea**.
(a)

Please tell me **whether you like it or not**. It is very important to me to know **what you think**.
(b) (c)

7. I can't remember **whether my grandparents have a computer**. I think
(a)

**that they have one**, but I don't know **wether they think it's a good invention or not**.
(b) (c)

8. I was wondering **how this works**. Actually, I can't really figure out **what is it**, and I don't
(a) (b)

know **who invented it**.
(c)

**2** Find and correct the mistakes in the information sheet about the Inventor's Fair.

---

**Inventor's Fair – Judge's Information**

It's time again for the Inventor's Fair. Thank you for being a judge. Please keep these things in mind when you judge the projects.

* It doesn't matter what age ~~is~~ the inventor ^is^. Anyone can win.

* If you don't know what is the invention, read the description.

5 * Test the invention to see either it works or not.

As you test each invention, ask yourself these questions to help you pick a winner.

* Can anyone figure out how the invention works?

* Can you tell wether or not the invention would be useful in daily life? Whom

would it help?

10 * Do you know wether the invention is unique or not? Does it already exist?

* It shouldn't matter either or not you like it. Judge the invention on if it is a good

idea or not. How useful is it to people?

* The inventors read your comments either they're good or bad. If you don't like

the invention, please write your comments politely.

---

# Self-Assessment

Circle the word or phrase that correctly completes each sentence.

1. I wonder _____ restaurant first sold a sandwich.

a. whether      b. what      c. when

2. I can't remember _____ invented the digital camera.

   a. who      b. if      c. that

3. I don't know what _____ about the new product.

   a. says      b. is saying      c. to say

4. I decided _____ to market my invention.

   a. how      b. what      c. if

5. You shouldn't forget _____ why you invented that.

   a. that      b. if      c. about

6. Do you know where _____ the information?

   a. finds      b. to find      c. if find

7. They don't care _____ or not that invention works.

   a. why      b. whether      c. if

8. I can't figure out _____ this invention works.

   a. what      b. which      c. if

9. I don't know whether to buy an older phone _____ the newest model.

   a. or      b. if      c. and

10. I haven't _____ whether or not to get a patent for my invention.

    a. remembered      b. decided      c. mattered

11. We should forget about _____ people will buy this and just create what we want.

    a. whether      b. if      c. or

12. _____ who invented the televison?

    a. Can you tell me      b. I was wondering      c. I don't know

13. _____ how to make a camera.

    a. Can anyone tell me      b. Do you know      c. I need to find out

14. Are you trying to find out _____ ?

    a. where the inventor      b. where the inventor is      c. where is the inventor

15. Do you know _____ ?

    a. whether his invention      b. did his invention      c. if did his invention
       won first place                win first place               win first place

# Direct Speech and Indirect Speech

## Human Motivation

## Direct Speech

**1** Complete the article with *asked* or *said.*

It is important to be motivated at work, and people have done a lot of research that shows what motivates employees. We wanted to know, however, what makes people feel *unmotivated* at work. We interviewed several experts in the field, and we

_asked_ , "What makes people feel unmotivated about
  (1)

their jobs?" Dr. Luiza Brito _____ , "Boredom[1]
                    (2)

makes people very unmotivated." Dr. Nicholas Peters agreed. He _____ , "People
                                                       (3)

are not motivated to do their jobs well when they become bored with the things they are

supposed to do." Eight of the ten experts we asked had a similar opinion. "When people

don't feel challenged,[2] they are not motivated to do their best," _____ Andrea Ledger,
                                                               (4)

an author and motivational speaker.

"Whose fault is it when employees aren't motivated?" we _____ . "Is it the
                                                              (5)

employees' fault or is it management's[3] fault?" Dr. Brito _____ , "It's management's
                                                                  (6)

fault. Employers need to find ways to motivate their employees." Dr. Peters had a slightly

different opinion. "It's the responsibility of both the employees and the employers to

make sure people are motivated," he _____ . Ms. Ledger had yet another opinion. She
                                                         (7)

_____ , "Why should managers motivate us?" When we expressed surprise at her
  (8)

question, she _____ , "Not all work is fun and interesting. Employees need to find
                    (9)

ways to motivate themselves no matter what the work is."

---

[1]**boredom:** a state of being uninterested | [2]**challenged:** given an interesting or difficult task to do | [3]**management:** the people
who run a company

**2** Read the conversation. Then rewrite the sentences in bold as direct speech, showing who said or asked them. The information in parentheses shows you where to put the reporting clauses – at the beginning, in the middle, or at the end of the sentences.

**Kyle:** Hey, everyone. I read this interesting article about motivation. It made

me think about what motivates me. Now I have a question for you.

**What motivates you to get out of bed in the morning?**
(1)

**Jing:** **Breakfast motivates me to get up, and I always look forward to a cup of coffee.**
(2)

**Dana:** **Nothing motivates me to get out of bed!**
(3)

**Kyle:** Very funny, Dana! Ian, **what about you?**
(4)

**Ian:** **The sunrise motivates me.** I like to take pictures of it.
(5)

**Kyle:** **It's interesting that everyone's answer was different.**
(6)

**Jing:** Hey, Kyle, **what about you? What motivates you to get out of bed?**
(7)

**Kyle:** **The Internet!** I like to read articles online when I get up in the morning.
(8)

1. (beginning)

     *Kyle asked, "What motivates you to get out of bed in the morning?"*

2. (middle)

   _____

3. (beginning)

   _____

4. (end)

   _____

5. (end)

   _____

6. (beginning)

   _____

7. (beginning)

   _____

8. (end)

   _____

**3** Unscramble the sentences about motivation. Use direct speech and add all the correct punctuation. Sometimes more than one answer is possible.

1. you / at work / what / motivates / Dan asked

   *"What motivates you at work?" Dan asked.* OR *Dan asked, "What motivates you at work?"*

2. Carol said / helps me / exercising during lunch / at work / stay motivated

   _____

3. motivated / keep me / at work / my deadlines / said Erica

   _____

4. a waiter / so I'm / said Josh / motivated / by tips / I'm

   _____

5. Rafael said / hard / motivates me / my manager / to work

   _____

6. don't need / I'm / external motivation / said Alison / because / I / naturally motivated

   _____

7. to get up / in the morning / said Chris / motivates me / my job

   _____

8. at your job / difficult / to find / Max asked / is it / motivation

   _____

# Indirect Speech

**1** Rewrite each quote as indirect speech. Use a reporting verb and change the main verb in each quote to express a past time.

> **Julie Mattes:** "The class is very motivating."
> **Greg Thompson:** "The students learned about the 19th century."
> **Debbie Morris:** "History is an interesting subject."
> **Dan Ito:** "The teacher is talking about inspiring leaders on Tuesday."
> **Laila Bhati:** "The class is going to a history museum."

## Review: History 101

We asked people about several classes at Thomson Community College.

Here's what students said about History 101. Julie Mattes, a history

major, *said that the class was very motivating* . Greg Thompson
                          (1)

_____ . Debbie Morris, who
                          (2)

is an English major, _____ .
                                              (3)

We asked students what topics the class covered. Dan Ito gave an example.

He _____ .
                          (4)

The students not only learn in the classroom, but they also often go on trips.

Laila Bhati _____ . Students clearly
                                        (5)

enjoy this class at TCC.

**2** Read the sentences about Dr. Andrews's advice to Marc O'Hallaran, a professional tennis player who has broken his arm. Then circle the word or phrase that completes each sentence with indirect speech.

1. Dr. Andrews said, "You have to do exercises so your arm can heal."

   He said that Marc _____ exercises so that his arm_____ .

   a. might do . . . can heal    (b. had to do . . . could heal)    c. had . . . might heal

2. Dr. Andrews said, "You shouldn't play tennis for at least eight weeks."

   He said that Marc _____ tennis for at least eight weeks.

   a. shouldn't play       b. might play       c. ought to

3. Dr. Andrews said, "You may be able to lift light weights after six weeks."

   He said that Marc _____ light weights after six weeks.

   a. can lift       b. might be able to lift       c. won't be able to lift

4. Dr. Andrews said, "You will need to work a long time to be 100 percent recovered."[1]

   He said that Marc _____ a long time to be 100 percent recovered.

   a. must need to work       b. would need to work       c. should work

---
[1]**recovered:** completely well, no longer injured

5. Dr. Andrews said, "You must work hard, and you have to stay motivated."

He said that Marc _____ hard, and that he _____ motivated.

a. might work ... could stay    b. could work ... could stay    c. had to work ... had to stay

6. Dr. Andrews said, "You ought to ask your trainer to help you focus."

He said that Marc _____ his trainer to help him focus.

a. asked        b. was going to ask        c. ought to ask

# Indirect Speech Without Tense Shift

**1** Read the advice people gave Brian about how to stay motivated at work. Then rewrite the bold sentences as indirect speech. Use *said* in the reporting clause and the same verb form as the direct speech in the reported sentence. Change the pronouns and use names when necessary.

**Brian:** I need help. **I'm having a problem staying motivated at work**. What should
                                                              (1)
I do?

**Diego:** **There are many ways to remain motivated during difficult times at work**.
                                                              (2)
Be creative!

**Joe:** I agree with Diego. **I avoid distraction by not checking my e-mail all day**.
                                                              (3)

**Tong:** Joe has a good point. **Checking e-mail wastes a lot of time**.
                                                              (4)

**Brian:** Thanks, everyone, but **I don't check e-mail very often at work**. Any
                                                              (5)
other ideas?

**Adam:** I was having problems staying motivated on the project I'm working on now

because it seems so endless. Then **I broke my work down into small parts**.
                                                              (6)
It's really helping!

**Erin:** Make a calendar with your deadline on it so you have a goal to work toward.

**Calendars really help me stay on schedule**.
                                                              (7)

1. _Brian said that he's having a problem staying motivated at work._

2. _____

3. _____

4. _____

5. _____

6. _____

7. _____

**2** Complete the sentences with indirect speech. Write sentences that are true for you.

1. When I talk to my friends or colleagues about motivation, they say _____

_____ .

2. My English teacher usually says _____

_____ .

3. A good friend of mine always says _____

_____ .

4. People usually say _____ , and I agree with that.

_____ .

5. When people talk about motivation, they say _____

_____ , but I don't think that's always true.

6. When people are unmotivated, sometimes they say _____

_____ .

# Other Reporting Verbs

**1** Complete the sentences about a class assignment. Circle the correct reporting verbs.

1. Mr. Watson **(informed)**/ **explained** the class that they had to give speeches.

2. Chuck **confessed** / **notified** to Mia that he was nervous about giving his speech.

3. Mia **mentioned** / **told** Chuck that she was also nervous.

4. Mia's older sister **reminded** / **explained** to them that they didn't need to get nervous.

5. She **swore** / **informed** that Mr. Watson had always given good grades when she was in his class.

6. She **convinced** / **replied** Mia and Chuck that they should relax before the speech.

**2** Complete the sentences about exercising. Rewrite the second sentence as indirect speech. Use names as the object after the reporting verbs, and add *to* when necessary. Sometimes more than one answer is possible.

1.  **Dan:** What's the best way to lose weight?
    **Kiran:** Every doctor has a different opinion!

    Kiran complained _to Dan that every doctor had a different opinion_ .

2. **Beatriz:** When I work out, I like to motivate myself by keeping track of my progress.
    **Paul:** Listening to music is also a good way to stay motivated.

    Paul mentioned _____ .

3.  **Ji Ah:** I just got an e-mail from the gym. I wonder what it's about.
    **E-mail:** The gym will be closed on Sunday.

    An e-mail notified _____ .

4.  **Cory:** I'm glad we both decided to exercise more. How is your exercise plan going?
    **Pablo:** It isn't going well at all.

    Pablo admitted _____ .

5. **Amanda:** This is hard. How can I stay motivated and keep running for another half hour?
    **Charlie:** The results will be worth it.

    Charlie assured _____ .

6.  **Anne:** Did anyone meet the weight loss goal?
    **Camila:** Jill lost ten pounds last month.

    Camila reminded _____ .

7. **Claire:** What is a good class to take for fitness?
    **Javier:** Yoga will help with fitness.

    Javier explained _____ .

# Avoid Common Mistakes

**1** Circle the mistakes.

1. I **admitted to Donna** that I didn't know what "boredom" meant. Donna **explained me**
   <br>      (a)                                                        (b)
   that "boredom" is what you feel when you're not interested in something or when there

   is nothing interesting to do. "Thank you for telling me," I **said**.
   <br>                                                                 (c)

2. Tom said, "**Martin Luther King, Jr. is** my greatest hero of all time." He also said that
   <br>                  (a)

   **Nelson Mandela inspired** him. He also said, **I met him on a plane five years ago**.
   <br>      (b)                                                  (c)

3. Jocelyn said, **This motivational workshop is expensive**. She asked me,
   <br>                                 (a)

   "**Are you going to attend it**?" I told her that **I was going to**.
   <br>        (b)                                       (c)

4. Dustin said that **he has accomplished** a lot in life because he was self-motivated. He
   <br>                             (a)

   told me **he hadn't looked up to** any heroes at all. He said, "**I can't think** of anyone who
   <br>                (b)                                      (c)

   inspired me."

5. Janice and Bob **complained** that their son wasn't motivated. They **admitted to me** that
   <br>                      (a)                                        (b)

   he had no internal motivation. I **mentioned them** that they could motivate him with
   <br>                                        (c)

   rewards.

6. The motivational speaker said, "**Follow your dreams.**" She also said, **Goals are important**.
   <br>                                     (a)                                        (b)

   She explained that **making money should not be your only goal**.
   <br>                                    (c)

7. My grandfather **told me** to work hard. He **explained to me** that work is one of the most
   <br>                          (a)                          (b)

   important things in life. He also **admitted me** that it was important to have fun once in
   <br>                                             (c)

   a while.

8. "**Music motivates me,**" Mariana said, **when I'm feeling bored**. Then she asked me,
   <br>      (a)                                        (b)

   "**Do you listen to music for motivation?**"
   <br>                        (c)

**2** Find and correct the mistakes in the article about using music for motivation.

---

**Music for Motivation**

    Music can be very motivational. Dr. Olivia Halston said, " ^ Music can make difficult jobs seem easier." ^ She explained us that music affects the brain. She said that she have discovered that music makes the brain happy. We wanted to know how music motivates our readers, so we did an online survey to ask about their music habits over a one-month

5 period. Many readers said that they listen to music for motivation when they exercised during that time. For example, Lien, a 22-year-old nurse, said, I listen to music on my headphones when I exercise. She reported us that it made her workout go faster. Other readers admitted us that they listened to music when they did housework. Jack, a student, said that next Saturday he will probably play music by the Rolling Stones when he

10 cleaned the house. "It won't make cleaning fun," he said, but it will make it better.

---

# Self-Assessment

Circle the word or phrase that correctly completes each sentence.

1. Jenna _____ "Nelson Mandela inspires me."

   a. "said"    b. said    c. said,

2. Hanan said, "I listen to music when I _____

   a. run.    b. run".    c. run."

3. "I am not challenged at work," _____ "so I'm bored."

   a. said Eric,    b. said Eric    c. said Eric,"

4. "What music do you listen to when you clean the house?" Jane _____ .

   a. told    b. asked    c. admitted

5. Phil asked, _____ time is the motivational speaker coming?"

   a. What"    b. "What    c. what

6. Matt said, "I don't work well early in the morning."

   Matt said that he _____ well early in the morning.

   a. doesn't work    b. won't work    c. isn't working

7. The manager said, "Alex worked the hardest last week."

   The manager said that Alex _____ the hardest last week.

   a. will work    b. had worked    c. works

8. Maria said, "You can sign up for the talk on motivation online."

   Maria said that I _____ sign up for the talk on motivation online.

   a. could    b. might    c. had to

9. Liz said, "Augusta is the capital of Maine."

   Liz said that Augusta _____ the capital of Maine.

   a. is    b. had been    c. is being

10. Barbara said, "Most people in my office are not motivated anymore."

    Barbara said that most people in her office _____ motivated anymore.

    a. hadn't been    b. haven't been    c. weren't

11. I _____ that the race would be difficult.

    a. told to you    b. told you    c. told

12. Jill _____ that it was too hot outside to be motivated to do anything.

    a. remarked    b. reminded    c. informed

13. Larry _____ me that I should join a gym. He thinks I'll be more motivated to exercise regularly.

    a. complained    b. remarked    c. convinced

14. Zai _____ to us that the office would close so that all the employees could attend the talk on motivation.

    a. notified    b. assured    c. reported

15. The survey _____ that 80 percent of the people were not motivated by money.

    a. confessed    b. reported    c. replied

## Indirect Questions

**1** Read the conversation about product sales. Then label the indirect questions *T* (true) or *F* (false). Rewrite each false sentence to make it true.

**Ms. Ortega**: Our sales are very low this year. Does anyone have any ideas for ways to increase sales?

**Bin**: How low are our sales?

**Ms. Ortega**: They're 25 percent below last year's sales. We
5    need to think of creative methods to improve them.

**Marta**: Can we start selling our products online? I think that would increase sales.

**Ms. Ortega**: That's a good idea.

**Bin**: I agree. When would we be able to start selling items online? Do you think it
10    would take a long time to start online sales?

**Ms. Ortega**: I think it would take at least six months. What can we do to improve sales until then?

**Marta**: We can advertise online even before people can buy products online. Does the company have a page on a social media website?

15 **Ms. Ortega**: No, we don't, but that's a good idea. Who could create a page for us?

**Bin**: Do you remember Ed Jones? He used to work here in the IT department,[1] and now he works from home. We could hire him to help us.

**Ms. Ortega**: That's a great idea. Do you have Ed's contact information?

**Bin**: Yes, I do. I'll e-mail it to you after the meeting.

[1] **IT department:** Information Technology department; the group of workers at a company responsible for the company's computers

1. Ms. Ortega asked her employees if they knew why sales were low.

   _F_ _Ms. Ortega asked her employees if they had any ideas for ways_
   _to increase sales._

2. Bin asked how low their sales were.

   ___ _____

3. Marta asked if they could stop selling their products online.

   ___ _____

4. Bin asked where they would be able to start selling items online.

   ___ _____

5. Bin asked if Ms. Ortega thought it would take a long time to start online sales.

   ___ _____

6. Marta asked if the company had a page on a social media website.

   ___ _____

7. Ms. Ortega asked who could sell a page for them.

   ___ _____

8. Bin asked Ms. Ortega if she remembered Ed Jones.

   ___ _____

9. Ms. Ortega asked Bin if he knew Ed.

   ___ _____

**2** Unscramble the indirect questions.

1. he / if / had time / Fen asked / to talk / Jack

   _Fen asked Jack if he had time to talk._

2. unhappy / she / Fen / Jack asked / if / was / at work

   _____

3. until 6:00 p.m. / she / if / him / Fen asked / had to / work

   _____

4. she / a problem / Fen / if / Jack asked / had / with her work schedule

   _____

5. Jack / Fen asked / she / if / to pick up her children / could / leave early

_____

6. with her babysitter / she / Fen / had a problem / Jack asked / if

_____

7. would / work from home tomorrow / if / Fen asked / Jack / be allowed to / she

_____

**3** Rewrite the questions as indirect questions. Make any necessary changes to pronouns.

1. Jill asked Dan, "Are you still having problems with your computer?"

   _Jill asked Dan if he was still having problems with his computer_____ .

2. Dan said, "Yes, I am." Then he asked Jill, "What can I do about it?"

   Dan said he was and _asked Jill what he could do about it_____ .

3. Jill asked Dan, "Have you reported the problem yet?"

   _____ .

4. Dan asked Jill, "Where can I report the problem?"

   _____ .

5. Jill asked, "Have you talked to the IT department?"

   _____ .

6. Then Jill asked, "Do you want me to go with you?"

   _____ .

7. Dan said, "No. That's OK." Then he asked Jill, "Who is the manager of the department?"

   Dan said that it was OK. Then _____ .

8. Jill asked, "Do you know Andre?"

   _____ .

9. Dan said, "I do." Then he asked, "Do you want to get some lunch?"

   Dan said he did and then _____ .

**144**   Unit 18   Indirect Questions; Indirect Imperatives, Requests, and Advice

# Indirect Imperatives, Requests, and Advice

**1** Read the article about people's advice for thinking creatively. Then rewrite the statements in bold. Use infinitives and the reporting verb *said*.

---

### ☀ How to Think Creatively ☀

What are the best ways to think creatively? We asked people in different fields what their opinions were. This is what they said.

♦ "You never know when a good idea will come to you. **Carry a notebook and a pen at all times.** Then you can write down good ideas when you get them."
5  – *John Merchant, author*

♦ "**Listen to music.** It's a great way to open your mind." – *Mercedes Rivera, singer*

♦ "**Brainstorm ideas.** That's what I do when I need a creative solution to a problem."
– *Bob Hu, web designer*

♦ "I know one thing not to do. **Don't watch TV.** TV kills creativity!" – *Naresh Gupta,*
10  *photographer*

♦ "**Read as much as possible.** Books exercise your brain and help you think about things in different ways." – *Anne Lawrence, teacher*

♦ "**Don't sit at a desk all day.** If you can't think of a solution to a problem, go for a walk. When you come back, you'll see things differently." – *Rich Simpson, manager*

15 ♦ "I have a trick that really helps me. **Meditate for 20 minutes every day.** Meditation is relaxing and helps you be more creative in problem solving." – *Teresa McDonald, editor*

♦ "**Exercise at least four times every week.** Exercise helps you focus on what's really important and gets rid of stress." – *Sophie Aitchison, accountant*

20 ♦ "**Talk to friends and colleagues.** Sometimes they have ideas that can really work." – *Paul Medeiros*

---

1. John Merchant _said to carry a notebook and a pen at all times_ .

2. Mercedes Rivera _____ .

3. Bob Hu _____ .

4. Naresh Gupta _____ .

5. Anne Lawrence _____ .

6. Rich Simpson _____ .

7. Teresa McDonald _____ .

8. Sophie Aitchison _____ .

9. Paul Medeiros _____ .

**2** Read these sentences about the advice Dr. Taylor, an expert problem-solver, gives to people. Then rewrite Dr. Taylor's statements. Use *told* or *asked* with infinitives.

1. Claire told Dr. Taylor that she was upset with her employees. Dr. Taylor said, "You should try to be patient."

   *Dr. Taylor told her to try to be patient.*

2. Mike explained to Dr. Taylor that he was very stressed at work and couldn't sleep at night. Dr. Taylor said, "Don't drink soda or coffee after 11:00 a.m."

   _____

3. Josh and Eileen told Dr. Taylor that they weren't communicating about their problems very well. Dr. Taylor said, "You should write down your problems before discussing them."

   _____

4. Martin sent text messages to his friend while he was talking about his problem. Dr. Taylor asked, "Would you please stop using your phone?"

   _____

5. We told Dr. Taylor we couldn't agree on where to go for vacation. Dr. Taylor said, "Don't worry about small problems."

   _____

6. Chris asked Dr. Taylor if they could meet on Wednesday. Dr. Taylor asked him, "Could we meet on Thursday instead?"

   _____

7. Janet and Bob tried to ignore their problems instead of talking about them. Dr. Taylor said, "Don't ignore problems when they occur."

   _____

8. Stephanie explained to Dr. Taylor that she didn't like her job, but didn't know how to find another one. Dr. Taylor asked, "Have you looked online for job opportunities?"

   _____

9. Nayoung asked Dr. Taylor if he could send his bills to her insurance company. Dr. Taylor asked, "Could you talk to my receptionist about your bills?"

   _____

10. Larry and Denise didn't arrive on time for their appointments. Dr. Taylor told them, "You need to learn to manage your time better."

   _____

# Avoid Common Mistakes

**1** Circle the mistakes.

1. Our boss (asked us that we talk) about our problems. She **told us to work** together
   (a)                                                                    (b)
   to find alternative solutions to traditional problems, and she **told us to listen** to each
                                                                     (c)
   other's ideas with an open mind.

2. Sharon asked me **if I liked** to solve problems. She asked me **how I solved** them
                     (a)                                          (b)
   creatively, and then she asked me **did I ever have** a problem I couldn't solve.
                                      (c)

3. Mauricio **said to be** on time for the meeting. He **told us to bring** pen and paper, and he
              (a)                                       (b)
   **told we'd be** brainstorming.
     (c)

4. Mrs. Harris **asked did I want** to lead the meeting. She asked **if I had been** in charge
                 (a)                                                 (b)
   before. She was hoping I'd say yes, but she asked **who would do** it if I couldn't.
                                                       (c)

5. My friend Tom **told me to stop** complaining, and my brother **told my problems** were
                   (a)                                             (b)
   small. Then Julie **asked why I was** so upset.
                       (c)

6. Mr. Moore told the students **to do** their homework, and he said that **there were** 10
                                 (a)                                        (b)
   math problems. He asked **them that they solve** them creatively.
                            (c)

7. John asked Carol **why she was** late to the meeting. He asked her **did she have** a
                      (a)                                               (b)
   problem. She said she did have a problem, and he asked her **if he could** help.
                                                               (c)

8. The speaker **told to sit** down at the beginning of his presentation. During the
                 (a)
   presentation, he **asked a man** to be quiet. Finally, when he was finished speaking, he
                     (b)
   **asked us** if we had any questions.
     (c)

**2** Find and correct the mistakes in the article about jobs for creative people.

### Top Jobs for Creative People

Are you a creative person? Dr. Lydia Garcia, a counselor who helps people find jobs,

says ~~that we go~~ *to go* after the job of your dreams. Here are some great jobs for creative people.

**Interior Designer:** We asked interior designer Julie Newton did she think her job was

creative. She told that it was. She explained that interior designers need to be creative

5 with colors, patterns, and light.

**Photographer:** Photographers need to have a creative eye. We asked photographer

Cory Davis could he tell us the most important tip for being a good photographer. He said

that we be unique and not to do what everyone else does.

**Teacher:** Teachers have to think of creative ways to help students learn. Teacher

10 Debbie Morgan has 25 students. She says that she's always thinking of new ways to help

her students learn. She tells to do their best, and she helps them do it.

**Chef:** Good chefs are creative chefs. People like a variety of different kinds of foods. We

asked Chef Asami Tanaka did she think it was important to be creative in the kitchen. She

told that it was. She explained that people want food that tastes good, but they also want

15 it to look nice.

Are any of these jobs for you? Whatever you do, follow Dr. Garcia's advice. She said

that you find a job that's right for you.

# Self-Assessment

Circle the word or phrase that correctly completes each sentence.

1. Rob asked if we _____ the meeting on time.

   a. would starting      b. would start       c. to start

2. Catalina asked Hank if he _____ a problem at work.

   a. will have      b. could have       c. had

3. **A:** What did the IT tech just tell you? **B:** She asked if her colleague _____ my problem.

   a. fixes      b. to fix       c. had fixed

4. The president asked if I _____ a new manager yet.

   a. to hire    b. were hiring    c. had hired

5. My boss asked us _____ to read the company's report.

   a. not to forget    b. to not forget    c. forget

6. Juan asked Melanie _____ she had a pen.

   a. who    b. did    c. if

7. He asked us _____ write down our problems.

   a. if we to    b. if we would    c. if would we

8. My boss asked, "Who helped you solve the computer problem?"

   My boss asked me who _____ solve the computer problem.

   a. helped her    b. had helped us    c. has helped you

9. Valeria asked Lei _____ to discuss the problem.

   a. when wanted she    b. when she wanted    c. when did she want

10. Kelly asked _____ I wanted to be a photographer.

    a. to me if    b. that    c. me if

11. Our teacher asked us _____ together on the project.

    a. to work    b. we work    c. she worked

12. Tatiana said _____ her when she has a problem.

    a. not to help    b. to help not    c. not help

13. Erol asked _____ the meeting early.

    a. leave    b. to leave    c. he could leave

14. She _____ to everyone's ideas.

    a. asked to listen us    b. asked listen    c. asked us to listen

15. He _____ Ivan to help him.

    a. asked me    b. asked    c. said

# The Passive (1)

## English as a Global Language

---

## Active vs. Passive Sentences

**1** Read the sentences about a new English word used by some Spanish speakers. Label the sentences *A* (active) or *P* (passive).

1. __P__ English is spoken around the world.

2. _____ Sometimes nonnative speakers create new "English" words.

3. _____ The word *coolisimo* is being used by some English speakers whose first language is Spanish.

4. _____ *Coolisimo* means "very cool."

5. _____ The Spanish ending *-isimo* was added to the English word *cool*.

6. _____ The word *coolisimo* is spread by people who speak both Spanish and English.

7. _____ Most native speakers of English probably have not heard the word *coolisimo*.

8. _____ Is the word *coolisimo* understood by most native English speakers?

**2** Rewrite the sentences about the use of English around the world. Use the passive. Do not use an agent.

1. People in many places speak English for many reasons.

   *English is spoken in many places for many reasons.*

2. People use English at airports and train stations.

   _____
   _____

3. People type commands in English on computers.

   _____

4. People are writing e-mails in English.

   _____

5. People make announcements in English at international events.

   _____

6. People hear English songs in many places.

_____

7. How do people use English in your country?

_____

8. Are people conducting business meetings in English?

_____

9. Do the schools ask students to read English-language books?

_____

**3** Complete the article about Cyber-English. Use the present perfect form of the passive with the verb in parentheses.

Since the late twentieth century, a special term _has been used_ (use) by some people
(1)

on the Internet. The term _____ (call) Cyber-English. Cyber-English
(2)

is the use of English when talking about things related to computers and technology.

Often, words found in computer directions _____ (not translate)
(3)

into different languages. Instead, words _____ (take) directly from
(4)

English for use in the directions. English words such as *click*, *e-mail*, and *link* often remain

in these directions. As a result, these words _____ (learn)
(5)

by people around the world, perhaps without them even realizing it. The world

_____ (bring) closer together by the use of computers, and
(6)

Cyber-English is an example of this.

**4** Complete the article about English in India. Circle the correct forms of the passive.

Today, English (**is spoken**)/ **was spoken** in many parts of India, but that wasn't always
(1)

true. In the early 1800s, English **is not being used / was not being used** widely there. The
(2)

use of English became more common after India became part of the British Empire

in 1858. After that, in the late 1800s, English universities **are started / were started**. Since
(3)

then, English **has been spread / was spread** by the education system. Today, in addition
(4)

to the local languages, English **is also being taught / was also being taught** in most
(5)

schools.

At the state level, a number of languages **have been made / are made** official in India,
(6)
including Hindi, Bengali, Urdu, and Punjabi, but English has become a very important
language for communication in the country. Nowadays, English **is used / was used** for
(7)
private and business communication between speakers of different languages in India.
Business meetings **are being conducted / were being conducted** in English. And even
(8)
some government documents **are being written / were being written** in English.
(9)

**5** Read the article on the Manx language. Cross out the *by* + agent phrases in bold if the
information is not important or if the meaning of the sentence is clear without it.

For many years, Manx was spoken ~~**by people**~~
(1)
on the Isle of Man. In 1765, the Isle of Man was sold

**by the Duke of Atholl**. It was sold **by the Duke**
(2)                                          (3)
to the British. After that, English was used

**by more and more people** on the island. The Manx
(4)
language began to disappear. In 1961, it was spoken

**by fewer than 200 inhabitants**. People on the island
(5)
were concerned about the loss of their language. The

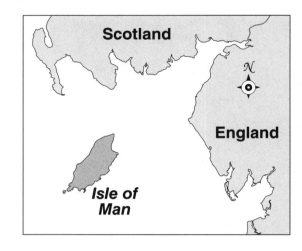

language was regarded **by the people** as an important part of their culture. In 1985, a
(6)
resolution was passed **by the government** to give Manx official recognition. More people
(7)
began speaking Manx, and it was taught **by teachers** in schools. By 2001, Manx was being
(8)
used **by over 1,500 people**, and today it is considered **by people** an important language
(9)                                                            (10)
again.

# Verbs and Objects with the Passive

**1** Read the sentences about the Latin alphabet. Label the sentences *T* (transitive) or
*I* (intransitive). Then rewrite the transitive sentences in the passive. Sometimes more than
one answer is possible.

1. __T__ English writers use the Latin alphabet.

   _The Latin alphabet is used by English writers._

2. _____ The Latin alphabet appears in written English, French, and many other languages.

   _____

3. _____ Many people around the world use the Latin alphabet.

_____

4. _____ The Latin alphabet started over 2,000 years ago.

_____

5. _____ The Romans created a writing system based on earlier alphabets.

_____

6. _____ Many letters in the Latin alphabet also appear in the ancient Greek alphabet.

_____

7. _____ In fact, the word *alphabet* comes from the first two letters of the Greek alphabet.

_____

8. _____ Eventually, the ancient Roman alphabet included 23 letters.

_____

9. _____ Many tourists to Italy easily recognize letters on ancient Roman monuments.

_____

**2** Read the sentences about a movie on the English language. Label the words in bold *DO* (direct object) or *IO* (indirect object). Then rewrite the sentences in the passive. Make the words in bold the subjects of the sentences. Sometimes more than one answer is possible.

1. _*DO*_ The teacher showed the class **a movie** about the history of English.

   *A movie about the history of English was shown to the class by the teacher.*

2. _____ The narrator told **the audience** the history of English since the fifth century.

_____

3. _____ The narrator offered the audience **examples of changes in the language over the centuries**.

_____

4. _____ The moviemakers showed **viewers** some of the varieties of spoken English.

_____

5. _____ English speakers from different places gave **the moviemakers** samples of speech.

_____

6. _____ The narrator showed **the differences between British English and American English**.

_____

# Reasons for Using the Passive

**1** Complete the steps for a language study. Use the simple past form of the passive with the verbs in parentheses.

**Step 1:** A survey <u>*was developed*</u> (develop) by language experts in Canada.
    <sub>(1)</sub>

**Step 2:** One hundred people _____ (include) in the survey about
    <sub>(2)</sub>
language. They were all from the province of Quebec.

**Step 3:** The participants _____ (ask) about what languages they
    <sub>(3)</sub>
spoke at home. About 80 percent answered French.

**Step 4:** The answers _____ (examine) by an expert. The expert
    <sub>(4)</sub>
found interesting results.

**Step 5:** The results _____ (compare) to results from a similar
    <sub>(5)</sub>
survey in New Brunswick. In New Brunswick, approximately 30 percent of people

speak French at home.

**Step 6:** The results and conclusions _____ (publish) in a report.
    <sub>(6)</sub>

**2** Look at a reporter's notes for a podcast. Then complete the podcast with the passive form of the verbs in the notes.

<u>Sign language</u>

1) A person is teaching sign language to chimpanzees at Lovitt Zoo.

2) The person has presented 20 words to the chimpanzees.

<u>Language survey</u>

3) An organization in our city conducted a survey last year.

4) Experts published the results last week.

5) People speak foreign languages more frequently than ever before.

<u>Most popular foreign language</u>

6) I made a mistake in my previous podcast.

7) I reported the most popular foreign language at Lovitt High School incorrectly.

8) More high school students are studying Chinese, not Japanese.

Hello. It's Tim Gradey with *Language News*. This is an interesting story.

Sign language *is being taught* to chimpanzees at Lovitt Zoo. Twenty words
(1)

_____ so far, and the trainer thinks the chimpanzees
(2)

are capable of learning many more.

Next, some fascinating results are in from a recent survey. A language survey

_____ in our city last year, and the results
(3)

_____ last week. The results show that foreign languages
(4)

_____ more frequently in our city than ever before, and
(5)

the trend is sure to continue.

Finally, a mistake _____ in my previous
(6)

podcast. The information about the most popular foreign language at Lovitt High

School _____ incorrectly. Chinese, not Japanese,
(7)

_____ by more high school students.
(8)

That's all for now. Tune in next time . . .

# Avoid Common Mistakes

**1** Circle the mistakes.

1. Portuguese **is spoken** in several countries around the world. It **is used** by more than
   (a)                                                                      (b)
   175 million native Portuguese speakers. My cousins (have been studied) Portuguese for
                                                          (c)
   five years.

2. What countries **is Portuguese spoken** in now? In the past, what countries
                    (a)
   **was it spoken** in? Why **it was made** the official language of Brazil?
       (b)                    (c)

3. English **is using** by approximately 330 million native speakers, and some people
              (a)
   estimate it **is used** by another 500 million nonnative speakers. It **is spoken** by
                  (b)                                                       (c)
   approximately 830 million people in total.

4. Chinese **is spoken** as a first language by over one billion people. Spanish **spoken** as a
              (a)                                                                   (b)
   first language by over 300 million people. As a first language, Arabic **is used** by over 200
                                                                              (c)
   million people.

5. The local languages **weren't used** at the business meeting. The meetings **conducted** in
   (a)                                                                                        (b)
   English. The speakers **were understood** by everyone.
                        (c)
6. That book **was written** in Japanese. It **is being translating** into several languages. It
               (a)                          (b)
   **is also being made** into a movie.
   (c)
7. Where **the movie was filmed?** **Was it made** in India? What awards
          (a)                       (b)
   **were the moviemakers given?**
   (c)
8. The movie **was made** in Canada. The actors **were spoken** French, so the producers
              (a)                                (b)
   **have included** English subtitles.
   (c)

**2** Find and correct the mistakes in the paragraph about English use around the world.

---

**English Your Way**

English is ~~use~~ *used* in many countries around the world. It is sometimes a difficult language

to learn. Pronunciation known to be difficult for some people. For example, the *j* as it is

pronouncing in English words (like *June*) can be difficult for Spanish speakers. That is

because the same sound does not occur in Spanish. Vowels are also difficult for most

5 learners of English. Many vowel sounds are finding in English. Americans are used about

fifteen vowel sounds. Also, the vowel sounds pronounced a bit differently in different

places in the English-speaking world. Learners have been found ways to improve their

pronunciation in English for a long time. Many pronunciation classes are offering at

schools. People also listen to native speakers to improve. What pronunciation tips you

10 were taught? Which ones are you using?

---

# Self-Assessment

Circle the word or phrase that correctly completes each sentence.

1. A survey about a global language _____ on a website.

   a. is be conducted      b. is being conduct      c. is being conducted

2. The word *smog* _____ by combining *smoke* and *fog*.

   a. was formed      b. form      c. be formed

3. Esperanto _____ today, but not by many people.

   a. is spoken     b. was being spoken     c. be spoken

4. The use of words in both Spanish and English _____ *Spanglish*.

   a. is calling     b. called     c. is called

5. People _____ to vote for the best choice for a global language.

   a. are being asked     b. is being asked     c. was being asked

6. Esperanto _____ in 1887.

   a. was developed     b. was develop     c. is being developed

7. A utensil that is like both a spoon and a fork _____ .

   a. is a *spork* called     b. is called a *spork*     c. a *spork* is called

8. New languages _____ without success.

   a. have often be developed     b. have often been developed     c. has often been developed

9. The website says that languages such as English, Spanish, and Esperanto _____ for the best global language.

   a. are considering     b. are being considered     c. considered

10. Many languages _____ at the international assembly.

    a. were being speaking     b. was being spoken     c. were being spoken

11. Esperanto _____ at a language conference I attended last year.

    a. were being spoken     b. is being spoken     c. was being spoken

12. Eurolang _____ in the 1990s as a language for the European Union.

    a. was creating     b. was create     c. was created

13. Eurolang was developed _____ .

    a. by     b. by Philip Hunt     c. Philip Hunt

14. Esperanto _____ to be an easy language.

    a. designed     b. was designing     c. was designed

15. The Pirahã language _____ many people.

    a. has never been spoken by     b. has never been spoken     c. has never be spoken by

# The Passive (2)

## Food Safety

---

## The Passive with *Be Going To* and Modals

**1** Complete the interview about genetically modified (GM) foods. Write questions with the words given. Then complete the two answers. Use the passive with *will*. An agent is not always necessary.

1. world hunger problems / solve / by GM foods

   **Interviewer:** *Will world hunger problems be solved by GM foods*?

   **Dr. Rivera:** Yes, they *'ll be solved by GM foods*. Countries can grow more of these crops.

   **Dr. Simms:** No, they *won't be solved by GM foods*. Better food distribution is the solution.

2. public concerns about GM food safety / reduce

   **Interviewer:** _____?

   **Dr. Rivera:** Yes, they _____.
   Up to now, there have been no incidences of illnesses from GM foods.

   **Dr. Simms:** No, they _____.
   The safety of GM foods has not been proven.

3. more and more GM foods / purchase / by consumers

   **Interviewer:** _____?

   **Dr. Rivera:** Yes, more GM foods _____.
   The foods are being sold in more places.

   **Dr. Simms:** No, more GM foods _____.
   People are going to buy more organic foods.

4. the safety of GM foods / confirm / by research

   **Interviewer:** _____?

   **Dr. Rivera:** Yes, it _____.
   Experts will be doing more studies.

   **Dr. Simms:** No, it _____.
   Studies will continue to show mixed results.

5. GM foods / regulate / more strictly / by more countries

**Interviewer:** _____ ?

**Dr. Rivera:** No, they _____ .
Many countries, like Great Britain, already have good regulations.

**Dr. Simms:** Yes, they _____ .
More countries are looking into the dangers of GM foods.

**2** Complete the introduction to a book about genetically modified food. Use the passive form of the verbs in parentheses with *be going to* or the present perfect. Sometimes more than one answer is possible.

## GM Food: Beware

### Introduction

The pros and cons of genetically modified (GM) food *have been discussed* (discuss) a lot over
_____(1)_____
the years, and the topic _____ certainly _____ (talk) about even more in the
_____(2)_____        _____(2)_____
future. The purpose of this book is to provide consumers with reliable information on what is already

known about GM food and its potential risks.

A lot of research _____ (do) over the past years on GM food, and
_____(3)_____
the results are usually not positive. For example, mice _____ (use)
_____(4)_____
in experiments on GM rice since 2008 in one laboratory. The experiments show the mice's

immune systems were damaged by eating the rice. These results tell us that it is possible people

_____ (harm) by GM rice in the future. This is only one example. Several
_____(5)_____
examples _____ (give) in this book that show other dangers of GM food.
_____(6)_____
More GM food research _____ (do) in the future, and it will likely
_____(7)_____
show more harmful effects of GM food. Some GM crops _____ (grow)
_____(8)_____
since the 1990s. They _____ (not test) properly or thoroughly, however,
_____(9)_____
they _____ (make) available for consumers. We still do not know all of
_____(10)_____
the effects of these products, but we know that in the future, it is quite possible that the negative

effects _____ (see) in people.
_____(11)_____
This book might not be read by the people who have the power to stop growing GM food, but I

hope that it will at least encourage the reader to stop consuming GM food.

**3** Complete the sentences about the pros and cons of GM foods. Use the passive form of the verbs in the boxes with the modals in parentheses.

**Pros**

| ~~grow~~ | keep | modify | sell |
|---|---|---|---|

1. GM crops _can be grown_ (can) without harmful pesticides.

2. GM foods _____ (may) to be much richer in nutrients[1] than they are now.

3. GM foods _____ (might) at lower prices if supermarkets pass cost savings on to consumers.

4. Some GM foods _____ (could) fresh longer if they were designed that way.

**Cons**

| cause | damage | know | test |
|---|---|---|---|

5. Harmful effects of GM foods on humans _____ (may not) yet.

6. Local environments _____ (could) by GM crops.

7. GM foods _____ (must) more thoroughly.

8. Health problems in humans _____ (might) by GM foods.

_____
[1]**nutrient:** a substance that is required by living things to live and grow

**4** Read the announcement from a conference on GM food. Then write opinions about the statements. Write sentences that are true for you. Use the passive with *should* (*not*).

> Good morning, and welcome to the Conference on GM Food. I'm going to start by telling you a few things that are going on in the field today.
>
> 1) Tests are being done on animals to find out the effects of GM food on humans.
>
> 2) GM crops are being sold before they are tested for long periods.
>
> 3) GM rice is being given to people in poor areas.
>
> 4) Identification labels are being put on GM products in supermarkets.
>
> 5) Brochures about the issues related to GM foods are being made available in supermarkets.

1. _____

2. _____

3. _____

4. _____

5. _____

# *Get* Passives

**1** Complete the podcast about food recalls. Use *get* passives in the simple present with the verbs in parentheses.

Welcome to the "Food Safety" podcast. Today, we're talking about food recalls. Food

<u>*gets recalled*</u> (recall) when it is dangerous to people. This means that stores can no
(1)

longer sell the product because there's something wrong with it. One major reason food is

recalled is because it _____ (contaminate) by a substance that will harm
(2)

people. Salmonella is one type of bacteria that makes food dangerous. It can be found on

meat that _____ (not cook) thoroughly enough. It's also found
(3)

on fruits and vegetables that _____ (not wash) properly. Another
(4)

reason food is recalled is because an object _____ (drop) into the food. For
(5)

example, plastic or paper could accidentally _____ (put) into a food item at
(6)

a factory. Most organizations take food safety seriously and recall items when they might

potentially harm the public. Be sure to tune in next week's podcast about safe food storage.

**2** Look at the chart about food being recalled. Then write sentences with *get* passives in the present progressive (for the food) and in the simple past (for the reason).

| | Product | Recalled | Reason |
|---|---|---|---|
| 1. | chicken | Yes | contaminated with salmonella |
| 2. | frozen potatoes | Yes | labeled incorrectly |
| 3. | fish | No | not contaminated |
| 4. | chocolate milk | Yes | not processed correctly |
| 5. | hot dogs | No | not damaged by bacteria |
| 6. | fruit drinks | Yes | not packaged correctly |

1. <u>*The chicken is getting recalled because it got contaminated with salmonella.*</u>

2. _____

3. _____

4. _____

5. _____

6. _____

**3** Read the interview with the owner of ChedCheese. Find seven more passive verbs and change them into *get* passives.

**Interviewer:** Last week, 1,000 cases of cheese made by ChedCheese, Inc. ~~were~~ *got* recalled. Today, the owner of ChedCheese, Mr. John Harris, is here to talk with us about the problem. Hello, Mr. Harris, and thank you for coming.

**Mr. Harris:** You're welcome. Thank you for having me.

5 **Interviewer:** So, tell us about the problem.

**Mr. Harris:** Well, several people became sick after eating our cheese, so all of our cheese products were tested by the FDA.

**Interviewer:** I see. And what did the FDA find?

**Mr. Harris:** They found that one of our cheeses had been contaminated.

10 **Interviewer:** So, what happened?

**Mr. Harris:** That cheese was recalled by the FDA. Of course, at ChedCheese, we are concerned about public safety. I personally made an announcement about the recall.

**Interviewer:** Do you know how the cheese was contaminated?

15 **Mr. Harris:** Yes, I do. Unfortunately, several of my employees did not follow our safety procedures.

**Interviewer:** And what happened to those employees? Were they fired?

**Mr. Harris:** Yes, I fired them. At ChedCheese, we take safety seriously.

**Interviewer:** Your company was shut down, right?

20 **Mr. Harris:** Yes, but it wasn't shut down by the government. I decided to close the factory and do a thorough cleaning of our equipment. We're going to reopen on Monday, and I want consumers to know it will be safe to buy our cheese again.

**Interviewer:** Thank you for your time, Mr. Harris.

# Passive Gerunds and Infinitives

**1** Complete the conversation with the correct passive form of the verbs in parentheses.

**Rob:** Hi, Sofia. Look at this article about unhealthy foods. Aren't you tired of

_being told_ (tell) what to eat all the time?
    (1)

**Sofia:** Not really. I like _____ (inform) about what is good and
    (2)

bad for me. For example, I learned that canned food can be really unhealthy.

One reason is that it has a lot of salt.

**Rob:** Yes, but when I read some of these food safety articles, I manage

_____ (persuade) that all food is bad!
    (3)

**Sofia:** Well, I guess you can't be afraid of _____ (harm) by all food,
    (4)

but you should avoid canned food.

**Rob:** I don't agree. Over the past few years, a lot of canned foods seem

_____ (improve) by food companies. They have a lot less
    (5)

salt and more nutrients. And sometimes it's just easier to heat something up than to

make it!

**Sofia:** Maybe, but some people complain about _____ (misinform).
    (6)

Sometimes companies make canned foods seem healthy when they're really not.

**Rob:** Well, I don't expect _____ (mislead) by every food label I read.
    (7)

Aren't there laws about giving false information on a food label? Besides, I don't think

it matters what you eat as long as you exercise. And eating canned food gives me more

time to go to the gym!

**Sofia:** Rob! Exercise isn't enough if you have an unhealthy diet!

**2** Complete the information from a brochure on food safety at home. Use *being* or *to be*.

1. People usually want _to be_ informed about food safety problems at home.

2. People who wash their hands regularly are less likely _____ infected by
germs in their kitchens.

3. People are usually interested in _____ shown how to prepare food safely.

4. Some people seemed _____ surprised to hear that the most commonly
contaminated food at home is meat.

5. Most people are concerned about _____ harmed by contaminated food in their homes.

6. Some people don't expect _____ harmed by the food that they buy.

**3** Complete the statements about food safety. Circle the correct words. Then check (✓) *Agree* or *Disagree* to show your opinion.

|  | Agree | Disagree |
|---|---|---|
| 1. **I expect /(I'm worried about)** being harmed by bad food. | ☐ | ☐ |
| 2. **I enjoy / I want** to be informed about food safety. | ☐ | ☐ |
| 3. **I hope / I avoid** to be told about food recalls. | ☐ | ☐ |
| 4. **I refuse / I'm afraid of** being exposed to germs in my kitchen. | ☐ | ☐ |
| 5. **I'm interested in / I seem** being educated about the food I eat. | ☐ | ☐ |
| 6. **I'm not likely / I'm afraid of** to be persuaded to buy unhealthy food. | ☐ | ☐ |

# Avoid Common Mistakes

**1** Circle the mistakes.

1. Many genetically modified (GM) animals **will probably be created** in the future. These
   (a)
   animals (**will be use**) to produce medicine. Many people **will be concerned** by this
   (b)                                                      (c)
   development.

2. Animals **can be created** to produce material for drugs that fight diseases in humans.
   (a)
   Some people think that these animals **should make** to help people. Others think that
   (b)
   people **could be harmed** by GM animals.
   (c)

3. The FDA **has put** restrictions on creating GM animals. A guide to how GM animals
   (a)
   are controlled **has been publish**. Some consumers **have been confused** about the
   (b)                                        (c)
   guidelines.

4. GM animals **might use** for food, too. All food from GM animals **is going to be checked**
   (a)                                                                    (b)
   by the FDA before it **can be sold**.
   (c)

5. Medicine made from GM animals **must be approved** by the FDA. The first medicine
   (a)
   **was made** from the milk from a GM goat. Patients **should tell** when their medicine is
   (b)                                          (c)
   created from a GM animal.

6. Some people think that medicines that were developed using GM animals

   **should not be approved** by the FDA. They think that these drugs **should be test** before
      (a)                                              (b)

   they are approved and their possible dangers **should be studied** for a longer period.
                                                 (c)

7. All medicines **should be tested** thoroughly before they are sold. Problems
                 (a)

   **can be found** with new medicines. Numerous tests **must perform** before new
     (b)                                       (c)

   medicines are sold.

8. Rules **should make** about labeling GM products before they go on the market. For
           (a)

   example, GM foods in supermarkets **could be labeled** with special stickers. Consumers
                                         (b)

   **should be informed** about all possible dangers from the very beginning.
           (c)

**2** Find and correct eight more mistakes in the paragraph about a local farmers' market.

---

**Community to Approve Farmers' Market**

                       *approved*
A farmers' market will formally be ~~approve~~ by the community board at its next

meeting. Farmers' products will be sell at a market downtown every weekend. The market

will be inspect by the health board before it opens in May. The health board needs to give

final approval. A wide variety of freshly grown products will be display for consumers

to choose, including fruits, vegetables, and flowers. In addition, products such as honey

might be include on the list of items available. GM foods won't sell at the market,

however. Cooking demonstrations may schedule for some weekends. More information

can find on the city's website. This market will be enjoy by families throughout the

community.

---

# Self-Assessment

Circle the word or phrase that correctly completes each sentence.

1. More food hybrids, crosses between two foods, _____ in the near future.

   a. will be developed      b. will be develop      c. will developing

2. GM foods should be _____ in supermarkets.

   a. label      b. labeled      c. labeling

3. Did the professor's paper on the benefits of GM foods _____ published?

   a. be      b. get      c. is

4. Broccoli and cauliflower can _____ crossed to produce "broccoflower."

   a. been      b. be      c. being

5. Organic foods are not likely _____ found at that supermarket.

   a. to be      b. be      c. being

6. More medicine from GM meats is _____ be created in the future.

   a. to go to      b. going      c. going to

7. Some people think food hybrids might be _____ more in the future.

   a. eat      b. eats      c. eaten

8. The article on pesticides _____ in the newspaper tomorrow.

   a. will not be published      b. not will be published      c. will not published

9. I'm concerned about _____ exposed to chemicals in my food.

   a. being      b. to be      c. be

10. Do you think these food labels could _____ ?

    a. understood      b. be understood      c. everyone be
       by everyone           by everyone            understood by

11. The scientists _____ to be given approval by the FDA.

    a. succeeded in      b. expected      c. missed

12. The proposal to develop GM fish _____ last week.

    a. got approved      b. got approve      c. approved

13.  _____ GM animals be raised on your farm?

   a. Do      b. Will      c. Are

14.  The animals on our farm _____ food with pesticides. We are aware of the potential risks.

   a. aren't feeding      b. are not going to feed      c. are not going to be fed

15.  _____ people be harmed by GM animals created for medicine? This is a good question for your debate.

   a. Do      b. Are      c. Could

# Subject Relative Clauses (Adjective Clauses with Subject Relative Pronouns)

## Alternative Energy Sources

## Identifying Subject Relative Clauses

**1** Read the paragraph about a family's use of geothermal energy. Underline the relative clauses and circle the nouns they refer to.

Helen and David Mitchell are (people) who live in Michigan. Michigan is a U.S. state that has very cold winters. In the winter, the Mitchells had heating bills which were over $600 a month. They did a lot of research to see how they could save money on their heating bill. Geotime is a company that installs a type of geothermal energy system. It is a system which is put underground. It uses heat from the ground to heat the home. Mr. Reynolds is a man who works for Geotime. He came to the Mitchells' house to explain the system, and they decided to have it installed. It has been very successful. In January, the Mitchells had a heating bill that was only $115!

**2** Complete the conversation about alternative energy sources in a community. Use the words in parentheses with the simple present.

**Luisa:** Are you interested in finding out about the types of alternative energy

_which are_ (which / be) available in our community? I belong to a group
(1)

_____ (that / help) the public learn more about green energy.
(2)

**David:** Sure. What options are available for people _____ (who / live) here?
(3)

**Luisa:** Well, there's wind energy. It's energy _____ (which / be) from
(4)

windmills. The power company _____ (that / run) the windmills
(5)

charges a little extra for the energy from them. There's also solar power. There are

many local companies _____ (that / install) solar panels.
(6)

**David:** Isn't the equipment _____ (which / collect) energy from the sun expensive?
(7)

**Luisa:** It can be. But solar energy pays off over time. Geothermal energy is a type of energy

_____ (which / save) people a lot of money.
(8)

**3** Rewrite the sentences about an environmental organization. Replace *that* with *which* or *who*.

1. The Clean Power Campaign is an organization that started over 20 years ago.

   *The Clean Power Campaign is an organization which started over 20 years ago.*

2. Clean Power Campaign was started by people that wanted to make a difference.

   _____

3. Clean Power Campaign employees talk to companies that use a lot of dirty fuels.

   _____

4. Employees that work for Clean Power Campaign encourage those companies to use renewable energy.

   _____

5. The organization contacts government agencies that make decisions about energy use.

   _____

6. Clean Power Campaign speaks to the agencies on behalf of citizens that are concerned about clean energy.

   _____

**4** Read part of a glossary of green energy terms. Then complete the sentences with relative clauses.

> **green:** a word describing something good for the environment
> **greens:** people supporting environmental organizations or political parties
> **green business:** a business selling products or services that do not harm the environment
> 5 **green-collar worker:** a person working for a green business or an environmental organization
> **green energy:** energy not harming the environment when produced or consumed
> **greenhouse gases:** gases trapping the sun's heat and causing a rise in
> 10   temperature

1. *Green* is a word _that describes something good for the environment_ .

2. *Greens* are people _____ .

3. A *green business* is a business _____ .

4. A *green-collar worker* is someone _____ .

5. *Green energy* is energy _____ .

6. *Greenhouse gases* are gases _____ .

# Nonidentifying Subject Relative Clauses

**1** Combine the sentences about green roofs. Make the second sentence a nonidentifying relative clause.

1. Green roofs help the environment. Green roofs are gardens on the tops of buildings.

   *Green roofs, which are gardens on the tops of*

   *buildings, help the environment.*

2. Energy costs can be reduced by green roofs. Green roofs keep heat out in the summer and keep heat in during the winter.

   _____

3. People put gardens on the tops of buildings. Gardens can include trees and flowers.

   _____

4. Trees and large plants are grown in one type of roof garden. This type of garden is also called an intensive roof garden.

   _____

5. Intensive gardens can seem like parks in the sky. The intensive gardens need a thick layer of soil.

   _____

6. Another kind of roof garden has low-growing plants in thin soil. This kind of garden is called an extensive roof garden.

   _____

7. My cousin grows carrots and peppers in his extensive garden. He is a professor researching green roofs.

   _____

**2** Write sentences with identifying or nonidentifying clauses. Use the sentence in bold to help you.

1. **I have two sisters with different jobs.**

   My sister / is a conservationist / is visiting tomorrow

   *My sister who is a conservationist is visiting tomorrow.*

2. **The type of car is additional information.**

   Ivan's car / is a hybrid / gets good gas mileage

   _____

3. **We have one uncle.**

   Our uncle / is an electrical engineer / has an electric car

   _____

4. **There are two companies called NRG in different locations.**

   The NRG / is located on Main Street / sells only eco-friendly products

   _____

5. **The number of employees is additional information.**

   Geotime / has 30 employees / installs geothermal systems

   _____

6. **Paulina works in two offices.**

   Paulina's office / is downtown / uses solar energy

   _____

# Subject Relative Clauses with *Whose*

**1** Complete the opinion letter to a newspaper. Circle the correct verbs. Then underline the nouns that the verbs agree with.

---

### *Vote on Energy* by Stephanie Price

We need to support leaders whose main <u>goal</u> **(is)** / **are** to use renewable energy sources.
(1)

Alex Nelson, whose <u>parents</u> **owns** / **own** a green company, is running for mayor. He works as a
(2)

lawyer at Crawford & Hu. Pat Crawford, who started the law firm and whose practice **is** / **are**
(3)

well known, helps preserve green spaces. Nelson's experience makes him a great candidate.

Rita Levins, whose volunteer activities in the community **is** / **are** numerous, is also
(4)

running for mayor. Levins, whose father **has worked** / **have worked** in a coal mine, supports
(5)

using coal as an energy source. She has served on the town council. Levins may be a

qualified politician, but she does not support renewable energy.

Jennifer Chen, whose campaign promises **includes** / **include** support for renewable
(6)

energy, is the third candidate for mayor. Chen, whose parents **owns** / **own** a gardening
(7)

business, has experience with green issues. However, Chen's main issue is support for

education, whose funding[1] **has been cut** / **have been cut**.
(8)

In my opinion, you should vote for Alex Nelson, whose experience **makes** / **make** him
(9)

the best person for the job.

---

[1]**funding:** money made available for a particular purpose

**2** Underline the relative clauses with *whose* in the sentences about building an energy-efficient home. Then label the relative clauses *I* (identifying) or *NI* (nonidentifying). Add commas to the sentences with nonidentifying relative clauses.

1. __NI__ Yesterday I spoke with my mother, whose cousin is Maria Sanchez.

2. _____ The Sanchezes are the family whose dream is to have an energy-efficient house.

3. _____ The Sanchez family are friends with someone whose company designs energy-efficient homes.

4. _____ Gloria Ramirez whose company is a family business will design their home.

5. _____ Gloria whose children all work in the business has two daughters and a son.

6. _____ Gloria's daughter whose specialty is eco-friendly home design will design the interiors.

7. _____ Gloria's son whose specialty is geothermal energy will install the heating system.

8. _____ These relatives of mine whose home is being built this year are pleased with the plans.

**3 A** Match the information about people and companies that won green awards to their actions.

1. __d__ Johanna Berenson, author     a. Her design for a green roof won an award.

2. _____ Laura Akpem, architect     b. His decisions led to cleaner energy for the city.

3. _____ Marcos Avilez, actor     c. Its windows are very energy-efficient.

4. _____ Eco-Car, a car company     d. Her books are about green energy.

5. _____ James Peters, politician     e. Its hybrid cars are some of the cleanest vehicles sold in the United States.

6. _____ Good Green Home Group, a remodeling company     f. His latest movie is about a worldwide energy crisis.

**B** Write sentences with the information from A. Use identifying subject relative clauses with *whose*.

1. _Johanna Berenson is an author whose books are about green energy._

2. _____

3. _____

4. _____

5. _____

6. _____

**4** Complete the review of a book about green homes. Use *who* or *whose*.

Johanna Berenson, *whose* newest book reached number one on the best-seller list
<sub>(1)</sub>

yesterday, has written several books on green energy. In her newest book, she gives advice

on how to have an energy-efficient home. Her advice is for homeowners _____ want
<sub>(2)</sub>

to reduce the amount of energy they use. Her book is also useful for people _____
<sub>(3)</sub>

want to build new homes that are green. Her book includes examples of people _____
<sub>(4)</sub>

homes are already green. It is full of information and tips that will help anyone _____
<sub>(5)</sub>

wants to go green get started. Whether you are someone _____ is new to green
<sub>(6)</sub>

building or someone _____ home is already green, you are sure to find useful
<sub>(7)</sub>

information in *Going Green: Home Edition*.

---

# Avoid Common Mistakes

**1** Circle the mistakes.

1. My parents, (**which**) believe in clean energy, have solar panels on their roof. Their house,
   <sub>(a)</sub>
   **which** is on a hill, gets a lot of sunlight. Their heating bill, **which** is sent monthly, is
   <sub>(b)</sub>                                                             <sub>(c)</sub>
   never very expensive.

2. I have a friend **who** is an electrical engineer. She works at a green energy company **that**
   <sub>(a)</sub>                                                                   <sub>(b)</sub>
   is in Denver. She has a job **who** is very difficult.
   <sub>(c)</sub>

3. Tina works at the farmers' **market, which is** only open on Saturdays. She passes out
   <sub>(a)</sub>
   **fliers that they are** about wind power. Her company hopes **people who take the fliers**
   <sub>(b)</sub>                                                           <sub>(c)</sub>
   will switch to wind power.

4. The person **who's** house is for sale is Mr. Lee. His sons, **who** don't live at home anymore,
   <sub>(a)</sub>                                                           <sub>(b)</sub>
   want to keep the house. The house, **which** has a green roof, is energy-efficient.
   <sub>(c)</sub>

5. In the future, we may have cars **which** run on biofuel. Imagine driving a car **who** runs
   <sub>(a)</sub>                                                                  <sub>(b)</sub>
   on oil from vegetables. Many plants **that** are rich in oil could be used for fuel.
   <sub>(c)</sub>

6. Matt is an **architect who he works** for a green company. His boss is a
   <sub>(a)</sub>
   **woman who cares** about the environment. The company's **houses, which are**
   <sub>(b)</sub>                                                           <sub>(c)</sub>
   eco-friendly, are expensive to build.

7. Claudia Rodriguez is a politician **who** is running for mayor. She is a person **that** has
   (a)                                                                        (b)
   been a lawyer in the past. She is someone **which** is concerned about dirty fuels.
                                               (c)

8. Kyle Morgan, **whose** father is an inventor, is trying to convert his house into an
                  (a)
   eco-friendly home. For example, he is trying to make a swimming pool **that** doesn't use
                                                                          (b)
   chemicals. His father, **who's** inventions have won awards, is helping him design it.
                           (c)

**2** Find and correct eight more mistakes in the article about making homes green.

---

**Go Green**
                                    *which* OR *that*
   There are many things you can do to have a home ~~who~~ helps the environment. Install

a solar panel system, which it heats your home with energy from the sun. You could

also get a geothermal system, who heats your home with energy from the ground. A

geothermal system, which it can be expensive at first, saves money over time. This type

5 of system, who heats your home cheaply, can also cool your home. You can find many

people online which sell solar panels and geothermal systems. You could also put a green

roof on your home. The roof, who helps to heat the home, can also be used for a garden.

Green roofs, which need to be flat, work best on new homes. Find an architect who's

company specializes in green roofs to build your home. There are many options for having

10 a home that it doesn't pollute the environment and saves you money on heating bills.

---

# Self-Assessment

Circle the word or phrase that correctly completes each sentence.

1. Wind turbines _____ are in fields near our town generate power for a lot of the state.

   a. whose       b. who       c. that

2. People _____ live in my town are not happy because they do not get much wind power.

   a. whose       b. which       c. who

3. Farmers who _____ windmills on their land want more wind power on their farms.

   a. has       b. have       c. to have

4. My friends Keith and Kristy have a home _____ uses solar power.

   a. whose       b. which       c. who

5. Some houses that rely on the sun's energy have large windows that _____ as solar panels.

   a. work      b. they work      c. works

6. _____ design green roofs have interesting jobs.

   a. People      b. People, who      c. People who

7. _____ installs solar panels, is opening his own business.

   a. Jerry Richards, who      b. Jerry Richards who      c. Jerry Richards, which

8. Maria Torrez, _____ is an urban planner, designed the green roof on our building.

   a. who      b. that      c. which

9. The roof of City Hall, which _____ plants and flowers on it, won a Green Award.

   a. have      b. has      c. it has

10. Mei Parks, _____ is running for mayor, supports renewable energy.

    a. which      b. whose      c. who

11. My friends, whose home _____ geothermal energy, have very low heating bills.

    a. use      b. is      c. uses

12. We're going to a concert _____ profits will be donated to a renewable energy fund.

    a. whose      b. which      c. that

13. My _____ has a green home. My other sister wastes a lot of energy.

    a. sister, who lives      b. sister who lives      c. sister whose lives
       in Portland,                in Portland                in Portland

14. Did you read the article _____ was about dirty fuels?

    a. who      b. whose      c. that

15. Our car, _____ great gas mileage, runs partly on electricity.

    a. that get      b. which get      c. which gets

# Object Relative Clauses (Adjective Clauses with Object Relative Pronouns)

## Biometrics

---

## Identifying Object Relative Clauses

**1** Read the description of a TV crime show. Then underline six more identifying object relative clauses and circle the nouns they refer to.

 *Forensic Files* is a popular TV show. It shows (crimes) that experts solve with forensic science. Each episode is about a different crime which someone has committed. In many episodes, investigators use DNA that criminals have left at
5 the crime scene to help them solve the case. Because each person's DNA is unique, the DNA that the investigators collect is often important evidence. Once investigators find a suspect, they can match the suspect's DNA to the DNA that they have found at the scene. The DNA can show if a suspect was present at a crime scene. However, DNA is not the only forensic
10 evidence that these investigators use to solve the crimes. They also use fingerprints, footprints, and even clothing fibers that they find at the scene. Investigators on the show usually use forensics to catch criminals, but not always. Some of the suspects who they investigate are innocent. Forensic evidence, like DNA, can help show that, too.

**2** Read the paragraphs about cold cases. Then cross out the relative pronouns that can be omitted.

 Forensics can be used to solve cases ~~that~~ police consider "cold." Cold cases are investigations **that** police have not been able to solve – sometimes for over 20 years.

 New technology **that** investigators didn't have in the past is available today, so crimes **which** people committed many years ago can eventually be solved. In one case, police
5 collected evidence from a crime **that** someone committed 30 years ago. The police found some hair at the crime scene, but the investigators couldn't prove **whose** hair it was. Thirty years later, the DNA in the hair **which** the police had found was tested. The hair matched one of the suspect's DNA, and he was arrested for the crime **that** he had committed years before.

 Cold case investigators have an important job. People **whose** family members criminals
10 have hurt may feel satisfied when a person is arrested even after many years.

**3** Combine the sentences in the descriptions of TV shows. Use identifying object relative clauses with *which* or *who*.

| TV show | Description | |
|---|---|---|
| 1. *Forensic Files* | Investigators use forensic evidence to solve crimes. Police find the forensic evidence at the crime scene. | |
| 2. *Most Shocking* | Terrible crimes are shown. People around the world have committed these crimes. | |
| 3. *Body of Evidence* | Dayle Hinman is an investigator. Viewers see her solve crimes with forensics. | |
| 4. *CSI* | Forensic investigators analyze data. The police find the data at the crime scene. | |
| 5. *Solved: Extreme Forensics* | Two unusual crimes are shown each week. Investigators solve the crimes with forensics. | |
| 6. *Body of Proof* | A medical examiner studies victims for evidence. She uses the evidence to solve crimes. | |

1. In *Forensic Files*, _investigators use forensic evidence which police find at the crime scene to solve crimes_ .

2. In *Most Shocking*, _____ .

3. In *Body of Evidence*, _____ .

4. In *CSI*, _____ .

5. In *Solved: Extreme Forensics*, _____ .

6. In *Body of Proof*, _____ .

# Nonidentifying Object Relative Clauses

**1** Rewrite the sentences about Robert A. Leonard and forensic linguistics. Make the sentences in parentheses nonidentifying object relative clauses that add information about the words in bold.

1. Robert A. Leonard was in **the band Sha Na Na**. (People loved it in the 1970s.)

   *Robert A. Leonard was in the band Sha Na Na, which people loved in the 1970s.*

2. Leonard became interested in **linguistics**. (He now teaches it at a university.)

   _____

3. He enjoys teaching **forensic linguistics**. (He describes it as the newest tool in investigations.)

   _____

4. Leonard thinks that **language** is like a fingerprint. (Each person uses it in a unique way.)

   _____

5. **Leonard** can often identify people by how they write. (Police sometimes ask him for help.)

   _____

6. **Leonard** has helped the police solve many crimes. (*Forensic Files* once interviewed him.)

   _____

**2** Combine each pair of lines of the conversation into one sentence. Make Nick's sentences into nonidentifying object relative clauses.

1. **Claire:** Sherlock Holmes is one of the most famous fictional detectives.

   **Nick:** Sir Arthur Conan Doyle created that character in the 1800s.

   *Sherlock Holmes, whom Sir Arthur Conan Doyle created in the 1800s, is one of the most famous fictional detectives.*

2. **Claire:** The first Sherlock Holmes mystery was *A Study in Scarlet*.

   **Nick:** People liked it immediately.

   _____

3. **Claire:** Holmes's most famous detective cases involved forensic evidence.

   **Nick:** He solved them with the use of logic.

   _____

4. **Claire:** Dr. Watson was Holmes's friend and assistant.

   **Nick:** Doyle uses Dr. Watson as the narrator for most of the stories.

   _____

5. **Claire:** In 2009, Robert Downey, Jr. played the detective in the movie *Sherlock Holmes*.

   **Nick:** Millions of people around the world saw it.

   _____

# Object Relative Clauses as Objects of Prepositions

**1 A** Complete the interview with an author of a mystery book. Use the correct relative pronouns. Sometimes more than one answer is possible.

**Interviewer:** Now for our *Book It* interview. Today we will speak to author Janice Jameson from Miami. She has written the best-selling book *Stranger Than True*, ✓ _which_ (1) I told you about before the break. So, tell us a little bit about your book, Janice.

**Janice:** Well, it's a fictional story about a murder that a detective named Martin is trying to solve. He arrives at a house _____ someone broke (2) into and finds very few clues.

**Interviewer:** Can you give us an idea how he solves the crime?

**Janice:** I can't tell you who the criminal is, but I can tell you Detective Martin finds a dog hair, _____ other investigators did not pay attention to. (3) This one dog hair is tested by forensic experts and helps him solve the crime.

**Interviewer:** Interesting . . . Your book, _____ you must have done research (4) on, is very realistic. Where did you find your information?

**Janice:** I have a cousin _____ I spoke with. He works in a forensic lab (5) in Miami. He gave me a lot of information about a case _____ (6) he worked on.

**Interviewer:** So, is there a real person _____ the main character is based on? (7)

**Janice:** Yes. Detective Martin is actually based on my husband!

**Interviewer:** Really? Is he a detective?

**Janice:** No, he's a teacher! Detective Martin's personality, _____
(8)

reviewers usually comment on, is like my husband's.

**Interviewer:** Well, it's a great book that I'm sure our audience will enjoy. Detective Martin

is an interesting character, and the forensics used to solve the crime are

fascinating. Thank you, Janice.

**B** Look at the conversation in A again. Place an **X** above the relative pronouns that can be omitted. Place a check (✓) above the relative pronouns that are necessary.

**2** Read the movie description. Then rewrite it with the prepositions before the relative pronouns when possible.

## Conviction

The movie *Conviction*, which Hilary Swank stars in, was released in 2010. Betty Anne Waters is the real-life woman who the movie is based on. Betty Anne fights to prove her brother is innocent of a murder that he was convicted of. She enters law school, which she graduates from after years of study. She is determined to prove her brother is innocent of the crime that others say he is guilty of.

*The movie Conviction, in which Hilary Swank stars, was released in 2010.*

_____

_____

_____

_____

_____

_____

# Avoid Common Mistakes

**1** Circle the mistakes.

1. A forensic tool **in which linguistics is used** is author identification. Experts,
   (a)
   (who police hire them), analyze threatening letters and e-mails. They compare the
   (b)
   threatening messages to other messages **that people have written**.
   (c)

2. Voice identification, **who** investigators use to solve crimes, is a forensic technique.
   (a)
   Threatening messages **that** criminals leave on phones are analyzed. Investigators, **who**
   (b)                                                                              (c)
   victims contact, compare the messages to suspects' voices.

3. Wildlife **forensics, which** many people are just learning about, is a new field. It uses
   (a)
   **animal DNA, which** wildlife forensic scientists analyze. Many **crimes, that** criminals
   (b)                                                              (c)
   commit against animals can be solved with its use.

4. **John, whose** father I work with at the police station, is studying forensics. He's taking
   (a)
   classes in forensic methods, **which** his father also studied. His father is a **person, whom**
   (b)                                                                            (c)
   John admires.

5. Donald Allison, **which** police caught at an airport, stole two rhinoceros horns. He was
   (a)
   getting on a plane with a fake antique piece **in which** the two horns were hidden. He
   (b)
   was arrested for the crime, **which** he had to spend one year in prison for.
   (c)

6. *CSI: New York*, **which** Gary Sinise stars in, is a TV show about forensic investigators. The
   (a)
   show, **what** many people enjoy watching, is about crimes and the investigators who
   (b)
   solve them. Sinise plays Detective Mac Taylor, **whom** the other investigators respect.
   (c)

7. TV shows **in which investigators use forensic evidence to solve crimes** have become
   (a)
   very popular. Criminals **who police arrest for crimes without forensic evidence**
   (b)
   are often not found guilty in trials. People on juries now expect forensic evidence,
   **which police cannot always find it** at a crime scene.
   (c)

8. Julia, **whose** taste in TV shows I admire, enjoys watching real-life stories. TruTV, **which**
   (a)                                                                                      (b)
   she watches every night, is a station with shows about crimes. The shows **what** Julia
   (c)
   likes watching the most are about forensics.

**2** Find and correct the mistakes in the article about the history of forensics.

> ### The History of Forensics
>
> *which*
> Forensic science, ~~who~~ many investigators use to solve crimes today, is not a new
> science. Fortunatus Fidelis, which people call the founder of forensic medicine,
> already practiced this type of medicine in the 1590s. Forensic medicine, what uses
> medical evidence to solve crimes, has changed over the years. Here are some historic
> 5 developments:
>
> 1. Fingerprints, which criminals leave them at crime scenes, became a way to identify
>    people in the late 1800s. However, computer systems what police use to scan, store,
>    and compare fingerprints weren't created until the last half of the twentieth century.
>
> 2. In 1901, Karl Landsteiner discovered that people have different blood types. After
> 10  that, investigators could use blood samples that they found them at crime scenes to
>    eliminate suspects.
>
> 3. In the 1980s, Ray White identified important features of DNA, who investigators now
>    collect from almost every modern-day crime scene. In 1987, DNA was first used to
>    prove that a man, who police thought had committed a crime, was guilty.
>
> 15  Technology in forensic science is always being developed, and there will be even more
>    ways, that police can catch criminals in the future.

---

# Self-Assessment

Circle the word or phrase that correctly completes each sentence.

1. Detectives are people _____ I admire.

   a. whose     b. who     c. which

2. Crimes _____ police couldn't solve in the past can sometimes be solved by using DNA.

   a. whose     b. who     c. that

3. My aunt, _____ I really respect, works in a forensics lab.

   a. whom     b. which     c. what

4. The investigators who the company _____ couldn't find any clues.

   a. hired them      b. hired      c. hired to

5. The victims _____ house the criminal broke into live on my street.

   a. which      b. whose      c. who

6. _____ people have studied for years, is now a degree program at some universities.

   a. Forensic science, which      b. Forensic science that      c. Forensic science, what

7. My favorite crime _____ many people watch, is *CSI.*

   a. show, which      b. show, who      c. show, that

8. That is the window that the criminal left his fingerprints _____ .

   a. them      b. whose      c. on

9. Detective Grendall, _____ Ted gave a statement, will handle the investigation.

   a. to who      b. to whom      c. to which

10. Police investigated the crime _____ was a witness.

    a. to which my brother      b. which my brother      c. to whom my brother

11. The apartment _____ was renting was robbed.

    a. what I      b. who I      c. I

12. The book *Crime Labs of the Future,* _____ I read for class, was about new forensic technology.

    a. whose      b. who      c. which

13. The witness, _____ , was late to the trial.

    a. who the defense      b. whom the defense      c. on which the
       relied                  relied on                  defense relied

14. Did you hear about the new book _____ the famous forensic anthropologist wrote?

    a. to whom      b. that      c. who

15. Investigators analyzed the letter _____ the murderer left at the crime scene.

    a. whose      b. what      c. which

# 23 Relative Clauses with *Where* and *When*; Reduced Relative Clauses

## Millennials

## Relative Clauses with *Where* and *When*

**1** Complete the beginning of an article about Generation Z. Use *where* or *when*.

### Generation Z

The United States is a country <u>*where*</u> people are often defined by their
(1)
generation. Generation Z is the youngest generation in the United States. Many

experts agree that the 2000s is the period _____ people in this generation were
(2)
born. This is a time _____ young people were exposed to a lot of technology. For
(3)
this reason, Generation Z is also called the *Internet Generation*. The Internet is the

place _____ many people in Generation Z "live." They communicate with each
(4)
other, play games, and do many other things on the Internet. They live in a world

_____ face-to-face communication isn't always necessary. Experts predict that
(5)
when people in Generation Z get older, it will be a time _____ many people will
(6)
work from home with computers.

**2** Rewrite the sentences about Gen Xers, people born between 1965 and 1981. Use the simple present of *be*, relative clauses with *where*, and the words in parentheses.

1. Gen Xers tend to enjoy spending time in coffee shops. (places)

   Coffee shops <u>*are places where Gen Xers tend to enjoy spending time*</u>.

2. Gen Xers have introduced many new ideas on the Internet. (place)

   The Internet _____.

3. Many Gen Xers shop at Amazon.com. (website)

   Amazon.com _____.

4. Gen Xers like to go on adventure vacations in countries like Chile and Nepal. (locations)

   Countries like Chile and Nepal _____.

5. Gen Xers want to work at companies with opportunities for promotion. (places)

   Companies with opportunities for promotion _____.

**3** Read the sentences about Internet use. Circle the relative clauses that are correct.

1. The 2010s are a time . . .  (in which many people use the Internet at home and at work.)

   which many people use the Internet at home and at work.

2. The Internet is a place . . .  where many young people communicate.

   that many young people communicate.

3. The 1990s were years . . .  when Internet use spread rapidly.

   during when Internet use spread rapidly.

4. South Korea is a country . . .  where most homes have Internet connections in.

   in which most homes have Internet connections.

5. This is the season . . .  in which most Internet applications start to sell.

   which most Internet applications start to sell.

# Reduced Relative Clauses

**1** Rewrite the sentences about generations. Use participle phrases and prepositional phrases. For adjectives, put the adjective before the noun.

1. Traditionalists are people who were born before 1946. They are people who are respectful.

   *Traditionalists are people born before 1946. They are respectful people.*

2. Baby Boomers are people who are optimistic. Most of them are people who are in their 50s and 60s.

   _____

   _____

3. Gen Xers are people who were born in the 1960s and 1970s. Gen Xers are people who are flexible.

   _____

   _____

4. Millennials are people who are looking for challenges. They are people who are educated.

   _____

   _____

**2** Combine the sentences using appositives. Make the second sentence the appositive.

1. Tim Scott is a Gen Xer. He is a sociology professor at Clark Community College.

   _Tim Scott, a sociology professor at Clark Community College, is a Gen Xer._

2. His son is a Gen Zer. He is a two-year-old.

   _____

3. Tim is doing research on China's Generation Y. China's Generation Y is the Chinese post-1980s generation.

   _____

4. Tim found out about Generation Y from Michael Stanat. Michael Stanat is the author of *China's Generation Y: Understanding the Future Leaders of the World's Next Superpower*.

   _____

5. According to Stanat, China's Generation Y is composed of approximately 200 million individuals. China's Generation Y is an entrepreneurial and tech-savvy group.

   _____

**3** Look at the picture of a conference about Millennials. Then combine the sentences with sentences in the box. Use participle or prepositional phrases. Sometimes more than one answer is possible.

| | |
|---|---|
| He is writing name tags. | She is speaking first at the conference. |
| It is on the information table. | ~~The conference is titled "Millennials in the Workplace."~~ |
| She is passing out the bottles of water. | The people are attending the conference. |

1. The people are attending a conference.

   _The people are attending a conference titled "Millennials in the Workplace."_

2. The organizers think that most of the people are Millennials.

   _____

3. There is a man at the information table.

   _____

4. The water is for the attendees.

_____

5. There is a woman by the information table.

_____

6. The woman is already on the stage.

_____

# Avoid Common Mistakes

**1** Circle the mistakes.

1. The United States is a **country where people are** often defined by their generation. It
   (a)
   is a **place where changes are** always happening. It is a **place where accept** change
   (b)                                                        (c)
   willingly.

2. The 1950s was the decade **when** the Beat movement started. It was a time **in when**
   (a)                                                                        (b)
   writers criticized many things about society. It was a period **in which** poets wrote
   (c)
   personal and political poems.

3. My aunt, **a Baby Boomer**, has had the same job for 30 years. My cousin, **a Millennial**,
   (a)                                                                       (b)
   has had three jobs. My brother, **is a Gen Zer**, wants to work at home.
   (c)

4. Tech Serve is a café **where people can use the Internet**. It is also a place
   (a)
   **where can have great food**. The chair **in which I like to sit** is near the window.
   (b)                               (c)

5. 1920 to 1945 is the period **in when the Traditionalists were born**. 1946 to 1964
   (a)
   is the period **that the Baby Boomers were born in**. 1965 to 1981 is the time
   (b)
   **when Gen Xers were born**.
   (c)

6. John F. Kennedy, **was the president of the United States from 1961 to 1963**, was
   (a)
   popular with Baby Boomers. Jack Kerouac, **who was a Beat Generation writer**, was
   (b)
   also popular with them. The Beatles, **a famous British band**, influenced many Baby
   (c)
   Boomers.

7. U2, **a band from Ireland**, is popular with Gen Xers. Bono, **is the lead singer for U2**,
   (a)                                                                    (b)
   writes most of the lyrics to their songs. The Edge, **who is the guitar player for U2**,
                                                        (c)
   writes a lot of the music.

8. 1929 is the year **when** the stock market crashed. 1963 is the year **in which** President
                    (a)                                                  (b)
   Kennedy died. 1989 is the year **in when** the Berlin Wall fell.
                                   (c)

**2** Find and correct seven more mistakes in the article about generation gaps.

---

**Generation Gap**

A generation gap is a difference in values and attitudes between two generations.
Sociologists, ~~are~~ people who study society, often examine generation gaps. The United
States is a country where have found gaps among generations.

The 1960s was a decade in when there was a big generation gap between

5 Traditionalists and Baby Boomers. Traditionalists, were the parents of the Baby Boomers,
were conservative. Their children, were the Baby Boomers, wanted to express their
personal freedom. It was a period in when the younger generation protested against
society and government. Big cities were places where often gathered to protest, sometimes
through music. Joan Baez, was a folk singer, sang protest songs. Many Traditionalists did

10 not like, or even understand, the music their children were listening to.

---

# Self-Assessment

Circle the word or phrase that correctly completes each sentence.

1. The United States is a _____ where there is a lot of interest in defining generations.

   a. year      b. time      c. country

2. The Pew Research Center is a place _____ research is being done on generations.

   a. where      b. when      c. which

3. A 2008 Pew Internet & American Life Project survey showed that 30 percent of
   adults _____ the Internet were Millennials.

   a. using      b. who using      c. are using

4. Heather often does research on the computers _____ the library.

    a. where      b. in      c. which in

5. The Internet is a place _____ teenagers and young adults go to communicate with friends.

    a. in where      b. when      c. where

6. The 1930s was a time _____ many people were unemployed.

    a. when      b. in when      c. where

7. The 1930s was the period _____ the Traditionalists grew up.

    a. where      b. which      c. in which

8. The United States is a _____ many popular Internet sites began.

    a. country where      b. country when      c. country

9. Many members of Generation X, _____ *Gen Xers*, helped created the Internet as we know it.

    a. who called      b. called      c. were called

10. Japan is a country _____ very common.

    a. where the use of technology is      b. the use of technology is      c. where is

11. Kyle is one of the sociologists _____ generations for a government report.

    a. researching      b. who researching      c. is researching

12. Maria does all of the work _____ for the report.

    a. is required      b. that required      c. required

13. Gen Xers, _____ , make up 23 percent of people on the Internet, according to a 2008 Pew Internet & American Life Project survey.

    a. who now in their      b. now in their      c. are now in their
       30s and 40s          30s and 40s        30s and 40s

14. Joe's research shows Millennials are often _____ people.

    a. sociable      b. in which sociable      c. who are sociable

15. Millennials _____ with technology often socialize online.

    a. are familiar      b. who familiar      c. familiar

# Real Conditionals: Present and Future

## Media in the United States

---

## Present Real Conditionals

**1** Complete the sentences about becoming a photojournalist. Use present real conditionals with the simple present form of the verbs and the words in parentheses.

1. If _you do not want_ (you / not want) to work in an office every day,

   _photojournalism is_ (photojournalism / be) a great career.

2. If _____ (you / be) a fair and ethical photojournalist,

   _____ (you / show) what you see and don't try to manipulate

   the image.

3. A _____ (photo / be) good when _____ (it / tell)

   a story without words.

4. _____ (you / need) to know how to use a variety of camera

   equipment if _____ (you / want) to be a photojournalist.

5. If _____ (someone / plan) to enter the field of photojournalism,

   _____ (there / be) many schools with strong programs.

6. When _____ (you / look for) a job or internship in the field,

   _____ (you / need) a portfolio of photos.

7. Often _____ (a person / not need) a photojournalism degree if

   _____ (he or she / have) a good portfolio.

8. Usually, _____ (people / try) to get assignments from news

   organizations if _____ (they / want) a job in the field.

9. If _____ (you / be) present at a major or interesting event,

   _____ (you / have) a chance to get a good photo to sell to a news

   organization or to add to your portfolio.

**2** Write sentences about citizen journalism. Use present real conditionals with *if* and the information given. (The symbol → points to the main clause.) Write each conditional once with the *if* clause first and once with the main clause first. If a noun is repeated in the two clauses, use a pronoun in the second clause.

1. you are not a trained journalist and you report a story → it is called "citizen journalism"

   *If you are not a trained journalist and you report a story, it is called*
   *"citizen journalism."*
   *It is called "citizen journalism" if you are not a trained journalist and you*
   *report a story.*

2. an average person submits a news story → a news organization considers the story

   _____

   _____

3. the story is interesting → a news organization often uses the story

   _____

   _____

4. the news organization is good → the news organization checks the facts

   _____

   _____

5. the stories are not objective → a good news organization does not use the stories

   _____

   _____

**3** Complete the conversation about news habits. Use present real conditionals with the words in parentheses and the simple present form of the verbs.

**Valeria:** How do you usually get the news?

**Tracey:** Well, I like to read the paper in the morning, but sometimes I get up too late.

**Valeria:** When *you don't read the paper* (you / not read / the paper),
   (1)
   _____ (what / you / do)?
   (2)

**Tracey:** If I get up late, I usually listen to the news on the radio. I listen to it when I'm

   getting ready for work. There's a public radio station I really like.

**Valeria:** All right. And _____ (what / news sources / you / use)
   (3)
   if _____ (you / want / news on something specific)?
   (4)

Tracey: What do you mean?

Valeria: Well, you know, _____ (what / happen) if
(5)
_____ (you / want / to find out more about a story)?

Tracey: Oh, I usually look up news like that online. What about you?

_____ (what / be / your favorite news sources) when
(7)
_____ (you / want / to get more information)?
(8)

Valeria: I usually look up stories online, too. When _____
(9)
(my friends / post / interesting news stories) on social networking sites,

_____ (I / often / follow up) by finding similar articles
(10)
in news sources.

Tracey: When _____ (you / be / home after work),
(11)
_____ (you / watch / the news on TV)?
(12)

Valeria: Not very often. It's just so easy to get the news other ways.

Tracey: I agree!

**4** Complete the sentences about news with information that is true for you. Emphasize the
result by using *then*.

1. If I read the news online, _____ .

2. If there is a major story in the news, _____ .

3. If a story doesn't sound objective, _____ .

4. If my friends tell me about an important story, _____ .

5. If there are stories about natural disasters, _____ .

# Future Real Conditionals

**1 A** Complete the conversation about bands. Use future real conditionals and the correct
form of the verbs in parentheses.

John: The Ballyhoo Band is on the cover of *Music News*. They're playing at Brandow Center next

month. I really want to go. If I _*have*_ (have) the money, I _*'ll get*_ (get) a ticket this week.
(1)                              (2)

Maria: You'd better buy it soon or they'll be sold out. If you _____ (wait) too
(3)
long, you _____ (not get) good seats.
(4)

**John:** Would you like to go with me?

**Maria:** I'd love to, but I can't. My cousin is getting married that weekend. If I

_____ (not go), my family _____ (be) really upset.
　　　(5)　　　　　　　　　　　　　　　　　　(6)

**John:** Oh, is the wedding going to be here or in another city?

**Maria:** Well, it's going to be at the family country house, about an hour from here. The

wedding is going to be outside, so I hope the weather is good.

**John:** If it _____ (rain), what _____ they _____ (do)?
　　　　　　(7)　　　　　　　　　　(8)　　　　　　(8)

**Maria:** They say that if the weather _____ (be) bad on the day of the
　　　　　　　　　　　　　　　　　　　(9)

wedding, they _____ (put up) tents.
　　　　　　　(10)

**John:** Well, I hope it doesn't rain – for their sake and for the concert's.

**Maria:** Me too. By the way, the Rock and Roll Hall of Fame induction ceremony is on TV

tonight. Are you planning to watch it?

**John:** Oh, I forgot about it entirely! I may have to work late tonight. Oh well, if I

_____ (miss) it, I _____ (watch) it online later.
　　　(11)　　　　　　　　　　　　　　(12)

**B** Complete the sentences about the conversation in A. Use *even if* or *unless*.

1. _Unless_ John buys the tickets for The Ballyhoo Band concert soon, he won't be able to get good seats.

2. Maria won't be able to go to the concert _____ she wants to.

3. The wedding Maria is attending will be outside _____ the weather is bad.

4. _____ the weather is bad, they won't need tents for the wedding.

5. _____ John works late tonight, he will be able to watch the Hall of Fame ceremony online.

**2** Answer the questions with future real conditionals and information that is true for you. If you write more than one result for the condition in your answer, don't repeat the *if* clause.

1. If you buy a magazine this week, what kind of magazine will you buy?

_____

2. If you get home early, will you watch the evening news? If not, what will you watch?

_____

3. What sites will you visit if you are online tonight?

_____

4. If you read an interesting article, will you try to find out more about the subject?

_____

# Real Conditionals with Modals, Modal-like Expressions, and Imperatives

**1** Complete the sentences about product reviews. Circle the correct modals.

1. If you want to buy a product online, you **(should)** / **can't** read reviews of it first. They're very helpful.

2. If an item has only bad reviews, it **should / must** not be good.

3. You probably **shouldn't / can't** buy the item if most of the reviews are negative.

4. If an item has several good reviews, it **can't / could** be worth buying.

5. Even if the reviews are positive, you still **have to / shouldn't** be careful.

6. When you read the reviews, you **should / can't** do it carefully. Make sure the reviewers are unbiased.

7. If all the reviews are great, they **might / can't** be reviews written by employees of the company.

8. Unless you know the source, you **may / can't** always trust what you read.

**2** Unscramble the sentences about the rules for submitting an online review.

1. include your name / you / If you / submit a review, / must

   *If you submit a review, you must include your name.* _____

2. could / write a review, / If you / it / help other people

   _____

3. We / publish your review / if you / can't / don't include your name

   _____

4. has to / write a review for us, / be fewer than 100 words long / When you / it

   _____

5. should / you are not biased / if / Your review / include positive and negative feedback

_____

6. these rules / write a review, / When you / follow

_____

**3** Look at the pictures. Then complete the real conditionals in the reviews. Use modals or modal-like expressions with the verbs in the boxes. Sometimes more than one answer is possible.

☆ ☆ ☆

| ~~be careful~~ | decide | find | not buy |
|---|---|---|---|

**Good but Dangerous**

*by Ned Chapple*

Overall, this meat slicer is great. However, if you buy it you

_ought to be careful_ OR _should be careful_ . It is very sharp. If
(1)

you have children, you _____ it. However, it
(2)

does work very well. You _____ the product
(3)

very useful if you cut a lot of meat. In fact, it works so well that you

_____ to throw away your knives!
(4)

☆ ☆ ☆ ☆ ☆

| download | own | save | stop buying |
|---|---|---|---|

**Reading, Even Better**

*by Sheila Aitchison*

If you love to read, you _____ this
(5)

e-reader! It's easy to use, and you can fit a lot of books on it. If you

don't have much room at home, you _____
(6)

large, heavy books. Imagine the space you'll save! If you want to get

books quickly, you _____ books in a matter
(7)

of minutes. Books for the e-reader are often less expensive, so you

_____ money, too.
(8)

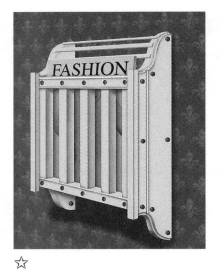

☆

| be | not get | not waste | improve |
|---|---|---|---|

**Magazine Attack**

*by Dan Brezinsky*

You _____ this magazine rack if
(9)

you want a product that works! It's terrible. If the design is

improved, it _____ a useful product.
(10)

As it is, it's hard to put together, and it doesn't hold many

magazines. The sellers _____ the product
(11)

if they want to get fewer customer complaints and returns. You

_____ your money on this low-quality
(12)

product.

☆ ☆ ☆ ☆

| be | not use | read | take up |
|---|---|---|---|

**A Good Buy**

*by Doris Searby*

This is a great lamp, but if you are very concerned about

the environment, you _____ it. You
(13)

can't use energy-efficient bulbs with it. It only takes regular

light bulbs. It is also very big. If you have a small desk, the

lamp _____ too much room on it. It
(14)

_____ OK for you if you have a large desk. It
(15)

is very attractive though, and it gives off a lot of light. If you are not

sure that this is the lamp for you, you _____
(16)

reviews of smaller, more environmentally-friendly lamps.

# Avoid Common Mistakes

**1** Circle the mistakes.

1. If you have a **smartphone, you** can get news updates on your phone. You can read the
   (a)
   news **quickly if** you get it on your phone. If you read an interesting news (story you) can
   (b)                                                                              (c)
   forward it to a friend.

2. **If you will want to be** a reporter, you will probably study journalism. **If you plan to be**
   (a)                                                                          (b)
   a photojournalist, you will learn to use a camera. **If you intend to be an editor**, you will
                                                       (c)
   need to be good at grammar.

3. If you don't read the newspaper, **how do you get** news? If you don't have a computer,
   (a)
   **where you will read** news stories? If you have a smartphone, **do you use** it to get
   (b)                                                              (c)
   news?

4. **If** the newspaper comes late tomorrow, I'll read it when I get home from work. **If** the
   (a)                                                                                  (b)
   newspaper comes on time, I'll read it during breakfast. **When** it snows a lot tomorrow,
                                                           (c)
   my newspaper won't be delivered at all.

5. If I help you with the article you're writing, **will you make** your deadline? If your editor
   (a)
   really likes your article, **it will be** published tomorrow? If your article is published,
   (b)
   **will your parents buy** several copies of the magazine?
   (c)

6. If people use social networking **sites they** sometimes post articles online. I often
   (a)
   include news **articles when** I post information online. Whenever I post something
   (b)
   **interesting, my** friends read the stories.
   (c)

7. It may rain, but **when** it's sunny tomorrow, we'll go to the parade. We'll take photos **if**
   (a)                                                                                         (b)
   we see anything interesting. We'll submit a photo to the school newspaper **if** we get a
                                                                              (c)
   good one at tomorrow's parade.

8. If **you take** a photo of an accident, send it to the police. If **the police get** the photo, it
   (a)                                                                (b)
   will help them find out facts about the accident. The police analysts will study the photo
   carefully if **they will get** it.
                (c)

**2** Find and correct the mistakes in the article about reading news on a smartphone.

> **News to Go**
>
> One way to get news is to get it on your cell phone. If people are on the go, they like
> to read the news wherever they are. If they have smartphones with Internet service they
> can usually read news anywhere. News companies are trying to make it even easier to
> get news on phones. If they will make news even easier to read on a small screen, more
> 5 people will read it.
>
> Companies consider several questions when they develop stories for cell phones. For
> example, if a story is long, people will read it? If people only will want to read stories on
> certain topics, how people can get these stories easily?
>
> If you will read or listen to the news on your phone, there could be some problems.
> 10 For example, imagine you are outside during your lunch break tomorrow, and you want
> to catch up on the news. When the weather is bad tomorrow, you probably won't get
> good cell phone service. You definitely won't use your phone outside when it rains a lot
> tomorrow. Of course, you wouldn't read a newspaper in the rain, either!

# Self-Assessment

Circle the word or phrase that correctly completes each sentence.

1. If you _____ the weather report, you will know what to wear tomorrow.

   a. will watch      b. watch      c. watching

2. If I _____ the news at 5:00, I watch the news at 7:00.

   a. will miss      b. missed      c. miss

3. Megan watches the news _____ her favorite reporter is on TV.

   a. whenever      b. unless      c. even if

4. If you always read the same _____ get different views on issues.

   a. news magazine,      b. news magazine      c. news magazine then
      you won't                you won't                 you won't

5. If a newspaper often prints sensational stories, _____ it?

   a. you read      b. do you read      c. you do read

6. If a citizen journalist writes a good story, _____ it has a chance of being used by a news organization.

   a. then      b. when      c. will

7. If you tell the truth, you _____ a problem.

   a. must have      b. had      c. won't have

8. If Diane quits writing for the magazine, _____ ?

   a. what she will do      b. what will she do      c. she will do

9. _____ the reporting gets better, I won't read that online news site again.

   a. Unless      b. If      c. When

10. If she's wearing a press badge, she _____ be a reporter.

    a. will      b. can't      c. must

11. My sister believes everything she reads _____ I tell her a story is not true.

    a. then      b. even if      c. if

12. If you read Jared's article, you _____ change your mind about the new economic policies. I did.

    a. can't      b. could      c. must

13. He shouldn't submit the _____ he hasn't checked the facts. He can't rely only on his sources.

    a. article, whenever      b. article, if      c. article when

14. If you want to be a reporter, _____ take journalism classes.

    a. you won't      b. you should      c. unless you

15. If my boss calls, _____ her I'm interviewing someone for my article.

    a. tell      b. should tell      c. will tell

# Unreal Conditionals: Present, Future, and Past

## Natural Disasters

## Present and Future Unreal Conditionals

**1** Complete the unreal conditionals with the verbs in parentheses. Use the simple past in the *if* clause. Use *would* in the main clause if it is a predicted result or *might* if it is a possible result. Use the information at the end of the sentences to help you.

**Brian:** If there <u>were</u> (be) a blizzard, I <u>wouldn't go</u> (not go) to work. (*predicted result*)
               (1)                      (2)

**Chris:** If we _____ (have) a blizzard, we _____ (stay) home.
                 (3)                          (4)
(*predicted result*)

**Mark:** If the city _____ (get) more than fifteen inches of snow, the mayor
                     (5)
_____ (close) the schools. (*predicted result*)
       (6)

**Peter:** If we _____ (not have) school, Matt _____ (catch up)
             (7)                       (8)
on his homework. (*possible result*)

**Gary:** If schools _____ (close), we _____ (not finish) our
             (9)                    (10)
group project in time. (*possible result*)

**Paula:** Claudia and Robert _____ (not drive) to the concert if there
                        (11)
_____ (be) a lot of snow on the roads. (*predicted result*)
   (12)

**2** Read the information in the chart. Then write unreal conditionals about the results of the natural disasters. Use *would* to express a predicted result. Use *could* to express a possible result. Sometimes more than one answer is possible.

| *If* Clause (condition) | Main Clause (result) | Result |
|---|---|---|
| 1. there / be / an earthquake | buildings / fall | Possible |
| 2. the forest fire / come / near town | residents / leave / their homes | Predicted |
| 3. there / be / a tornado | people / go / to their basements | Predicted |
| 4. it / rain / a lot | streets / flood | Possible |
| 5. there / be / a hurricane | houses on the beach / be / in danger | Predicted |
| 6. we / have / a heat wave | many plants / die | Possible |

1. _If there were an earthquake, buildings could fall._ OR _Buildings could fall if there were an earthquake._

2. _____

3. _____

4. _____

5. _____

6. _____

**3** Read the report on a meeting about school closings. Then rewrite the quotations in bold as present unreal conditionals. Make any necessary changes in wording.

    At the city board meeting on Friday, many people expressed their concerns about the number of snow days at local schools. Eric Sheffield, a concerned parent, said, "**The mayor cancels school constantly, so our students can't get a solid education.**" Mayor Jenkins responded, "**It snows frequently, so I have to cancel school.**" He added that if
5 more than six days are missed, they will be made up at the end of the year. Blanca Morales, a school teacher, said, "**We miss a large number of days, so we have to make them up at the end of the year.**" Mayor Jenkins responded, "**Safety is a priority, so I can't keep schools open during bad weather.**" Dan Park, a local businessman, mentioned that the city doesn't have enough equipment to clear all the roads for school buses. He said,
10 "**The city doesn't have good snow removal equipment, so we have a lot of canceled school days.**" Melanie Brooks, a city employee, said, "**The city doesn't raise taxes, so we can't buy new equipment.**" She added that people probably didn't want higher taxes. The discussion will continue at next month's meeting.

1. Eric Sheffield: _If the mayor didn't cancel school constantly, our students could get a solid education._

2. Mayor Jenkins: _____

_____

3. Blanca Morales: _____

_____

4. Mayor Jenkins: _____

_____

5. Dan Park: _____

_____

6. Melanie Brooks: _____

_____

**4** Look at the web article about things to do in Seattle and at the weather forecast for each day. Then write advice for tourists about each day of their vacation. Use present unreal conditionals. Sometimes more than one answer is possible.

## Things to Do in Seattle

- Take a city bus tour
- Hike Mount Rainier – Amazing volcano just 60 miles from the city
- Visit the Space Needle – Fantastic city views from the top on a clear day
- Take a ferry to the San Juan Islands – Beautiful wildlife just an hour from
5  Anacortes, which is about 80 miles from Seattle
- Go to the Museum of Flight – Entertainment and information for the entire family
- Shop at Pike Place Market – This indoor market has been selling the best local food for over 100 years
10 • Take an underground tour of Pioneer Square – A very interesting and unusual view of the city and its history

1. Monday

   *If I were you, I wouldn't visit the Space Needle.* OR *I would go to the Museum of Flight if I were you.*

2. Tuesday

   _____

3. Wednesday

   _____

4. Thursday

   _____

5. Friday

   _____

# Past Unreal Conditionals

**1** Read the sentences about a fire. Then answer the *Yes / No* questions.

1. If there hadn't been a heat wave, the fire wouldn't have started.

   a. Was there a heat wave? *Yes*

   b. Was there a fire? *Yes*

2. If the firefighters hadn't responded quickly, the fire would have spread to other buildings.

   a. Did the firefighters respond quickly? _____

   b. Did the fire spread to more than one building? _____

3. No one would have been injured if everyone had left the area.

   a. Did everyone leave the area? _____

   b. Was anyone injured? _____

4. Two people could have died if they hadn't been rescued in time by the firefighters.

   a. Were the people rescued in time? _____

   b. Did anyone die? _____

5. If the fire hadn't occurred during the day, a lot of people might have been injured.

   a. Did the fire occur during the day? _____

   b. Were a lot of people injured? _____

**2** Rewrite the sentences about the 2010 eruption of a volcano in Iceland. Use *if* to make past unreal conditionals.

1. Most people heard about the eruption because it disrupted a lot of flights.

   *Most people wouldn't have heard about the eruption if it hadn't disrupted a lot of flights.*

2. Flights didn't continue because the smoke and ash were so thick in the air.

   _____

3. Flights stopped because the pilots weren't able to see.

   _____

4. Many tourists didn't fly home because the airports closed.

   _____

5. The catastrophe affected so many countries in Europe because the wind was so strong.

   _____

**3** Look at the picture of a street after a storm. Then complete the past unreal conditionals. Use the verbs in the box. In the main clause, use *would* for predicted results and *could* or *might* for possible results. Sometimes more than one answer is possible.

| be | fall | not get | remember | slow |
|----|------|---------|----------|------|
| close | go | not step | see | stay |

1. The trash can _might not have fallen_ over if it _had been_ heavier.

2. If the driver _____ down, Alison

   _____ dry.

3. The car seats _____ wet if Bobby

   _____ the windows.

4. If Melissa _____ the puddle, she

   _____ in it.

5. The dogs _____ inside if someone

   _____ to let them in.

**4** Complete the conversation about what people did during a thunderstorm. Write indirect advice using past unreal conditionals. Write sentences that are true for you.

1. **A:** The power went out, and I sat in the dark for four hours!

   **B:** _____

2. **A:** I talked on my cell phone until the battery died.

   **B:** _____

3. **A:** I assumed the food in the refrigerator would stay fresh.

   **B:** _____

4. **A:** I went to bed and left the windows open.

   **B:** _____

5. **A:** I left some candles burning while I slept.

   **B:** _____

# Wishes About the Present, Future, and Past

**1** Complete the phone conversation. Use the simple past, past progressive, past perfect, *would*, or *could* with the verbs in parentheses.

**Annie:** I wish that I <u>*had seen*</u> (see) the tornado yesterday.
                                        (1)

 **Jorge:** I saw it while I was driving.

**Annie:** Really? That must have been scary.

 **Jorge:** It was. I wish I _____ (be) home during the tornado. But I'm
                                        (2)

       glad that I got home OK after it passed.

**Annie:** This weather has been crazy. I wish that it _____ (not rain) now.
                                                                        (3)

 **Jorge:** I know. I don't want to drive in this weather. I wish I _____ (not make)
                                                                                (4)

       plans to go out today.

**Annie:** Can you cancel them?

 **Jorge:** No. I have an interview this afternoon. I wish I _____ (reschedule)
                                                                        (5)

       it, but I can't.

**Annie:** What job are you interviewing for?

 **Jorge:** It's for a disaster recovery organization. I'd be answering phones. I wish that it

       _____ (be) a better job, but it's a start.
                                        (6)

**Annie:** Yes . . . you need to start somewhere. Then maybe you can get a promotion. I wish

my boss _____ (promote) me, but she won't.
<sub>(7)</sub>

**Jorge:** Could you ask her for a raise?

**Annie:** I wish that I _____ (ask) for a raise, but my company isn't giving
<sub>(8)</sub>

raises this year. Maybe next year. . . .

**Jorge:** Yes. It's good to have a positive attitude. Well, I wish I _____ (talk)
<sub>(9)</sub>

longer, but I can't. I need to get ready for my interview.

**Annie:** OK. Good luck. Call me back after the interview!

**2** Write sentences with *wish* to express the people's wishes and regrets.

1. I didn't take any pictures of the storm.

   *I wish (that) I had taken pictures of the storm.*

2. I left my umbrella at home.

   _____

3. I can't go outside and play soccer right now.

   _____

4. I hope the rain stops.

   _____

5. It rains every week here. I don't like it.

   _____

6. My rain boots have holes in them.

   _____

7. I can't go to the park today.

   _____

8. I like the winter. Then it snows.

   _____

# Avoid Common Mistakes

**1** Circle the mistakes.

1. If Paul **didn't work** with disaster relief, he wouldn't be so stressed. Also, if he **works**
   (a)                                                                                    (b)
   fewer hours, he would spend more time with friends. I really think that he would have
   more time in the day if he **got** a different job.
   (c)

2. We would watch TV **if the power were working**. We could listen to the radio **if had**
   (a)                                                                              (b)
   batteries. **If our phone were working**, we would call our family to say we are OK.
   (c)

3. Our office would have been destroyed if the architect **didn't design** it to withstand
   (a)
   earthquakes. I wish all the buildings in our city **had been built** as well as ours was. But
   (b)
   they were not. If the earthquake **had been** bigger, a lot of buildings would have fallen.
   (c)

4. I wish you **had seen** the storm. It was amazing! If I **charged** my camera batteries,
   (a)                                                   (b)
   I **could have taken** pictures to show you.
   (c)

5. If he **trained** better, he could have passed the test. If he **had passed** the test, he would
   (a)                                                        (b)
   have been a firefighter. His parents would have been proud if he **had become**
   (c)
   a firefighter.

6. If we **worked** together, we could make a difference. We could raise a lot of money if we
   (a)
   **chose** to work for the same charity. I would love it if we **work** together for survivors of
   (b)                                                            (c)
   the hurricane.

7. I wish you **called** me. If you **had told** me about the storm, I **would have come and stayed**
   (a)                     (b)                                    (c)
   with you.

8. **A:** If **I were** you, I would take an umbrella to work today.
          (a)
   **B:** I hate when it rains. It would be great if **I could leave** work early.
                                                    (b)
   **A:** If **you get** to work on time every day, it might be easier to leave early.
          (c)

**2** Find and correct eight more mistakes in the article about a survivor of a blizzard.

---

**Joe Simpson: Survivor**

         *weren't*
If it ~~isnt~~ for a tragic event, no one would know about Joe Simpson. In 1985, Joe

Simpson and Simon Yates were climbing a mountain in the Andes. If a blizzard didn't

happen, the trip might have ended without any problems. The two climbers got to the

top of the mountain, but they had problems on the way down. If it hadn't been icy, Joe

5 wouldn't have slipped. However, it was icy, and Joe slipped and broke his leg. He could

have climbed down the mountain if hadn't gotten the injury. Because Joe couldn't walk,

Simon lowered Joe down the mountain on a rope. When they were almost back to the

camp, Joe slipped again. He was dangling on the rope over the edge of the mountain. He

could have climbed up the rope if had had the strength. If the weather didn't damage

10 Simon's hands, he might have been able to pull Joe up. Simon held on to the rope for

several hours, but he finally had to cut the rope. He thought Joe had died, but Joe was not

dead. He had fallen more than 100 feet, but even with his hurt leg, he had managed to

climb to safety and get back to the camp.

        In 1988, Joe Simpson wrote a book, called *Touching the Void*, about the experience. If

15 the book wasn't a huge success, the movie about the climb might not have been made. I

wish that I did not see the movie before I read the book. I also wish I went to the movie

with a friend. It was frightening! Of course, it was inspiring, too. If I am you, I would rent

the movie today!

---

# Self-Assessment

Circle the word or phrase that correctly completes each sentence.

1. If I _____ how to ski, I would go skiing with you.

    a. know      b. had known      c. knew

2. If the roads weren't icy, I _____ worry about driving to work.

    a. didn't      b. wouldn't      c. could

3. She wouldn't go to school if she _____ sick.

   a. were    b. is    c. be

4. If it hadn't been so hot, the fire might not _____ .

   a. started    b. start    c. have started

5. I wouldn't go outside if I _____ you.

   a. could be    b. were    c. am

6. If the storm had been reported on the news, we _____ for it.

   a. are ready    b. might get ready    c. might have been ready

7. If it had snowed more, the city _____ the schools.

   a. closed    b. would have closed    c. would close

8. I _____ you about the storm if my phone had worked.

   a. will tell    b. would have told    c. told

9. If I hadn't been nervous, I _____ better during the interview.

   a. could have done    b. could do    c. did do

10. If I _____ you, I would have stayed in the basement during the storm.

    a. was    b. am    c. had been

11. If I _____ the training, I could have become a firefighter.

    a. had finished    b. have finished    c. could finish

12. I _____ that it would snow.

    a. wishing    b. wish    c. would wish

13. Janet wishes that she _____ her umbrella at home this morning.

    a. isn't leaving    b. didn't leave    c. hadn't left

14. I wish we _____ better disaster policies in our state. Can't our legislators do something about it?

    a. were having    b. have    c. had

15. Hai wishes he _____ snowboard. He wants to learn how.

    a. could    b. would    c. might

# Conjunctions

## Globalization of Food

## Connecting Words and Phrases with Conjunctions

**1 A** Look at the menu. Then complete the sentences. Use *and* or *or*. Sometimes more than one answer is possible.

### Dinner Special

*Choose one entrée and two sides.*
*Dinner also comes with a small salad or soup, a drink, and a dessert.*

**Entrées**

**Meat:** chicken, beef, lamb

**Fish:** salmon, tuna, shrimp

**Vegetarian:** eggplant, tofu

**Sides**

**Potatoes:** baked potato, French fries

**Vegetables:** corn, carrots, peas

**Drinks**

coffee, tea, soda

**Dessert**

chocolate cake, apple pie

1. For the dinner special, you can choose one entrée _**and**_ two sides.

2. You can choose a small salad _____ soup with the dinner special.

3. The dinner special comes with a drink _____ a dessert.

4. For the entrée, you can have meat, fish, _____ a vegetarian dish.

5. The eggplant _____ the tofu are vegetarian dishes.

6. For a side, you can choose a potato _____ a vegetable dish.

7. Coffee, tea, _____ soda are all drinks on the menu.

8. For dessert, you can choose the chocolate cake _____ the apple pie.

**B** Look at the menu in A again. Then complete the restaurant review. Use *and*, *but*, or *or*. Sometimes more than one answer is possible.

The restaurant Mango opened last month. The restaurant is spacious _**and**_ modern. The
(1)

restaurant is new _____ already popular. You need to call for reservations.
(2)

The food is inexpensive _____ delicious. The dinner special is the best value for
(3)

your money. It comes with an entrée, a small salad or soup, two sides, a drink, _____
(4)

a dessert. For the entrée, try the chicken _____ the eggplant. The chicken is really
(5)

spicy _____ not too peppery. The eggplant is mild _____ still tasty. Don't try the
(6)                                                        (7)

beef, the lamb, _____ the tuna. They're all overcooked. The one item you must have is
(8)

the chocolate cake. It's chocolaty _____ not too sweet!
(9)

**2** Complete the conversation between a waiter and a customer. Use *and*, *but also*, *nor*, or *or* with the simple present form of the verbs in parentheses.

**Waiter:** Can I take your order, or do you have any questions about the menu?

**Customer:** Yes. Do you recommend the salmon or the tuna?

**Waiter:** Both the salmon _**and**_ the tuna _**are**_ (be) delicious.
(1)                    (2)

**Customer:** Are they salty?

**Waiter:** No. Neither the salmon _____ the tuna _____ (be) salty.
(3)                      (4)

**Customer:** Well, I guess I'll have the tuna with a salad.

**Waiter:** Do you want the Greek salad or the house salad?

**Customer:** Either the Greek salad _____ the house salad _____ (be) fine. Which do you
(5)                            (6)

recommend?

**Waiter:** I prefer the Greek salad. As the menu says, "Not only the dressing _____ the cheese
(7)

_____ (add) to the taste of this customer favorite."
(8)

**Customer:** OK. That sounds good.

**Waiter:** Great. Do you want French fries or a baked potato?

**Customer:** To be honest, neither the French fries _____ the baked potato _____ (sound)
(9)                              (10)

good. Can I get something healthier?

**Waiter:** How about a vegetable? Both the corn _____ the carrots _____ (be) healthy.
(11)                          (12)

**Customer:** I'll have the corn. Thanks.

**3** Combine the sentences about two restaurants that serve *crêpes*, a kind of thin pancake. Use the correlative conjunctions in parentheses. Sometimes more than one answer is possible.

1. La Crêperie is a restaurant that serves crêpes. Sweet Spot is a restaurant that serves crêpes. (both . . . and)

   *Both La Crêperie and Sweet Spot are restaurants that serve crêpes.*

2. At the restaurants, you can have savory crêpes. At the restaurants, you can have sweet crêpes. (either . . . or)

   _____

3. The crêpes are inexpensive. They are large. (not only . . . but also)

   _____

4. The chocolate crêpes are delicious. The strawberry crêpes are delicious. (both . . . and)

   _____

5. Coffee is not free at La Crêperie. Tea is not free at La Crêperie. (neither . . . nor)

   _____

# Connecting Sentences with Coordinating Conjunctions

**1** Complete the paragraphs about a cooking show. Use *and*, *but*, or *so*. Only use *and* when no other conjunction is possible. Sometimes more than one answer is possible.

### The Globalization of TV

   *Iron Chef* was a TV show in Japan, __*and*__ it was very popular in the 1990s. On the show,
   (1)

two chefs would compete in each episode. One chef was an Iron Chef, the name given to

the chefs who were on the show repeatedly. The other chef was a guest chef. Both the Iron

Chef and the guest chef were given a type of food, _____ they had to make dishes
                                                       (2)

with that food as the main ingredient. The chefs usually used the main ingredient in four

dishes, _____ they sometimes cooked five or more dishes. The show was only an
         (3)

hour long, _____ the chefs didn't have much time to cook, _____ each of them
            (4)                                                    (5)

was helped by two assistants. Then judges ate the food. One of the judges was usually a

professional food critic, _____ the other judges were often just celebrities. The judges
                           (6)

scored the food, _____ the chef with the highest points won the competition.
                  (7)

*Iron Chef* ended in Japan in 1999, _____ reruns of the show were played in the
(8)

United States. The Japanese show became popular in the United States, _____ a U.S.
(9)

version called *Iron Chef America* was developed in 2005.

**2** Complete the sentences about Mexican food. Circle the correct conjunctions.

1. Authentic Mexican food has a lot of spices, **yet** / **and** it doesn't always taste very spicy.

2. There are some really spicy sauces, **but** / **and** they're not served with every dish.

3. Danielle loves cheese, **or** / **so** cheese enchiladas are her favorite dish.

4. Some diners always have enchiladas with a red sauce, **yet** / **so** it is possible to get them with a green sauce, too.

5. In Mexico, the beef tacos usually have shredded beef, **yet** / **or** they're made with steak.

6. In some Mexican restaurants in the United States and Canada, the food is quite different from the food served in Mexico, **yet** / **and** it is still advertised as Mexican.

**3** Read the article about international food. Rewrite these sentences with a compound verb. In some sentences, the subject or the subject + auxiliary verb does not need to be repeated.

## ❧ International Food ✎

Many cuisines are popular around the world. Look at our list of some of the most popular types of food around the world.

◆ There are many Greek restaurants around the world, and they are often owned by Greek people.

5 ◆ Chinese food is eaten everywhere, and it is our number-one choice for international food.

◆ Mexican food is popular, and it is enjoyed by people in many countries.

◆ Thai food can be found in many places, and it is usually similar to the food in Thailand.

◆ Italian food is found around the world, but the pizza is better in Italy!

10 ◆ Indian restaurants are common in England, and they are found in many other countries.

◆ You should try French food in France, and you should have it in Canada.

◆ Japanese restaurants are in many countries, and sushi is often on the menu.

1. *Chinese food is eaten everywhere and is our number-one choice for*
   *international food.*

2. _____

3. _____

4. _____

5. _____

# Reducing Sentences with Similar Clauses

**1** Complete the online message board comments about chain restaurants. Use the correct verb forms. Add *too*, *so*, *either*, or *neither* when necessary.

**Jake07:** I want to know what you think! Should people eat at American chain restaurants when they travel to other countries?

**Dond27:** No way! Chain restaurants are terrible in the United States, and the chain restaurants in other countries _are_ , _too_ .
(1)    (1)

**Maria52:** I disagree. The quality of chain restaurant food in the United States is good and dependable, and it _____ in Mexico, _____ !
(2)         (2)

**SG1987:** I agree with Dond27. I haven't had good food in chain restaurants here, and I _____ in other countries _____ .
(3)         (3)

**TOOTIE:** I'm with Maria52. I ate at a pizza chain in India. The pizza was terrific, and _____ _____ the atmosphere!
(4)      (4)

**KVN67:** I agree with Maria52, too. Once I ate at a fast-food restaurant in Switzerland. The burger was fantastic, and the potatoes _____ _____ . The
(5)      (5)
burger was fried, but the potatoes _____ . I think the potatoes were
(6)
baked. Good . . . and healthy!

**Friendlee:** Last year, I ate at a burger restaurant in France. The burger wasn't good, but the fries _____ . In fact, the fries were delicious!
(7)

**G3Harris:** I don't want to eat at chain restaurants when I travel, and _____
(8)
_____ my family! We like to try the local food.
(8)

**Rita2010:** I'm with G3Harris. I won't even eat in chain restaurants here in the United States, and my husband _____ _____ !
(9)     (9)

**Jake07:** Thanks, everyone. I'm enjoying reading your opinions, and _____ _____
(10)     (10)
my roommates! Please keep posting.

**2** Read a restaurant critic's rating chart about the main courses available in a restaurant. Then write two sentences for each statement. Use *too*, *so*, *either*, or *neither* with the words in parentheses.

|  | Expensive | Grilled | Good | Salty |
|---|---|---|---|---|
| **Chicken** | No | No | Yes | Yes |
| **Steak** | Yes | Yes | Yes | No |
| **Lamb** | Yes | No | No | No |
| **Fish** | No | Yes | No | Yes |

1. The chicken isn't expensive.

   (fish)   *Neither is the fish.*   *The fish isn't, either.*

2. The steak is expensive.

   (lamb) _____   _____

3. The lamb isn't grilled.

   (chicken) _____   _____

4. The fish is grilled.

   (steak) _____   _____

5. The chicken was good.

   (steak) _____   _____

6. The lamb wasn't good.

   (fish) _____   _____

7. The steak wasn't salty.

   (lamb) _____   _____

8. The fish was salty.

   (chicken) _____   _____

**3** Write sentences about restaurants with information that is true for you. Use two clauses and reduce the words in the second clause. Use *too*, *so*, *either*, *neither*, or *but*.

1. Burger restaurants / be / popular

   _____

2. I / like / French food

   _____

3. I / eat / fast food

_____

4. Italian food / be / popular

_____

5. Sushi / be / popular

_____

6. Salad bars / be / healthy

_____

7. Many people / don't like / spicy foods

_____

# Avoid Common Mistakes

**1** Circle the mistakes.

1. The restaurant serves Mexican **and** Central American food. It doesn't have TexMex food
   <br>(a)
   **and** food from Spain. You can't get *chili con carne* **or** *paella*.
   <br>(b)                                         (c)

2. Jorge wants to open **a restaurant, and he'd** like it to be downtown. He'll serve food
   <br>(a)
   in **the restaurant and have** a take-out service. He plans to borrow money from
   <br>(b)
   **his parents, and pay** them back.
   <br>(c)

3. The United States has a lot of Chinese restaurants, and Costa Rica does, **too**. The
   <br>(a)
   American restaurants don't always have traditional food from China, and the Costa

   Rican restaurants don't, **too**. The Americans have adapted some of the dishes, and the
   <br>(b)
   Costa Ricans have, **too**.
   <br>(c)

4. **Either** Italian food and French food are popular in the United States. Some Italian
   <br>(a)
   restaurants serve **both** authentic Italian dishes and Italian-American dishes. Some
   <br>(b)
   French restaurants serve **either** standard French dishes or dishes from different regions
   <br>(c)
   in France.

5. Bob's Pizza serves Americanized pizza, and Andy's does, **too.** Traditional Italian
   <br>(a)
   pizza doesn't have a thick red sauce, and it doesn't have thick melted cheese, **either.**
   <br>(b)
   Traditional Italian pizza doesn't have a chewy crust, and the crust isn't thick, **too.**
   <br>(c)

6. A *churrascaria* is a traditional Brazilian restaurant that is popular in **both** Brazil and the (a) United States. These restaurants have **either** a salad bar and all-you-can-eat meat. You (b) usually have a card at your table that you can turn to **either** red (stop serving) or green (c) (keep serving).

7. In my town, there isn't a Greek restaurant **and** a Thai one. We also don't have a Korean (a) restaurant **or** a Japanese one. We do have a Mexican restaurant **and** a Chinese one. (b)                                                                                     (c)

8. I love **Korean food but don't like** kimchi. It is too **spicy for me, and I don't like** the (a)                                              (b) flavor. Kimchi usually comes in **a separate dish, and is served** as a side. (c)

**2** Find and correct seven more mistakes in the article about fruit-growing regions.

---

### Oranges All Year Round

Places like Florida and California can grow fruit year-round, but places like New York and Minnesota cannot because the climate is too cold. For example, oranges do not grow *either* in cold climates, and lemons do not, ~~too~~. However, either oranges and lemons can be found in supermarkets all year round. Where do they come from? Most supermarkets in

5 places with cold winters import food from other places. Oranges are grown in California, and are shipped to places like New York.

There are some fruits that do not grow well in warm and cold climates in the United States. Therefore, many fruits are imported from other countries. For example, either Peru and Mexico export avocados to the United States. Durian is not native to the United

10 States, and passion fruit is not, too. Durian is often imported from Malaysia and Indonesia, and passion fruit is imported from New Zealand and Brazil. Lychee is another fruit that is not very common in the United States. It is grown in some areas of the United States, but is mainly imported from places like China. These exotic fruits usually cannot be found in small towns and smaller cities. However, supermarkets in bigger cities usually sell them.

---

# Self-Assessment

Circle the word or phrase that correctly completes each sentence.

1. I love to eat exotic fruits and _____ .

   a. vegetables    b. delicious    c. buy

2. Do you want to go to an Italian restaurant _____ a French restaurant for dinner?

   a. and    b. or    c. but

3. My local supermarket, which is owned by some Greek immigrants, imports fruit from Asia, Africa, _____ South America.

   a. and    b. or    c. but

4. Durian tastes delicious _____ smells awful.

   a. and    b. or    c. but

5. _____ mangoes and lychee are grown in India.

   a. Not only    b. Either    c. Both

6. Neither passion fruit nor oranges _____ in this area.

   a. grow    b. grows    c. to grow

7. This restaurant serves _____ traditional and adapted Korean dishes.

   a. both    b. either    c. neither

8. Durian is prickly on the outside, _____ the inside is soft.

   a. yet    b. or    c. nor

9. Our town is located near Mexico, _____ we cross the border to eat at authentic Mexican restaurants.

   a. or    b. but    c. so

10. We could order _____ get pasta.

    a. pizza so    b. pizza or    c. pizza, or

11. My sister loves _____ I don't like it.

    a. lychee, or    b. lychee and    c. lychee, but

12. My parents don't like to try food from other cultures, but I _____ .

    a. don't    b. do    c. neither

13. Chinese food is delicious, and _____ Chinese-American food.

    a. either is      b. so is      c. neither is

14. I have tried durian, and my brother _____ .

    a. too      b. has, too      c. hasn't, either

15. Paul doesn't drink coffee after a meal, and _____ .

    a. neither do I      b. I do neither      c. neither don't I

# Adverb Clauses and Phrases

## Consumerism

---

## Subordinators and Adverb Clauses

**1** Complete the article about saving money. Circle the correct subordinators.

I decided to find ways to save money **though** / (**because**) I was spending too much and
(1)

having financial problems. You may find these tips helpful **while / since** they worked
(2)

for me!

- I take a list with me **while / because** I'm shopping, and I buy only the items on the list.
(3)

- I opened up a savings account. **Although / As** I had a checking account, I had never
(4)

  had a savings account. Now I put money in it every month. **Even though / Since** I do
(5)

  not put a lot of money in it, the money adds up over time!

- I make a monthly budget. **While / Because** I have bills to pay every month, I
(6)

  write down what I need to spend every month on rent, food, and things like that.

  **While / When** it is still tempting to spend too much, I find that with a budget it is
(7)

  easier to resist spending urges.

- I cook at home more. I love to eat out, but I have done it less often **though / since**
(8)

  I realized I was spending too much at restaurants. I also take my lunch to work.

- I use a small part of my savings to go shopping once a month. **While / As** before I
(9)

  would waste money throughout the month, now I buy one item for myself at the end

  of the month.

  Good luck! I hope you can save money **even though / as** it's rewarding in the end!
(10)

**2** Look at the chart about how Americans spend money. Then complete the sentences with adverb clauses. Use the subordinators *although, because, even though, since, though, when,* or *while* with the correct percentages. Sometimes more than one answer is possible.

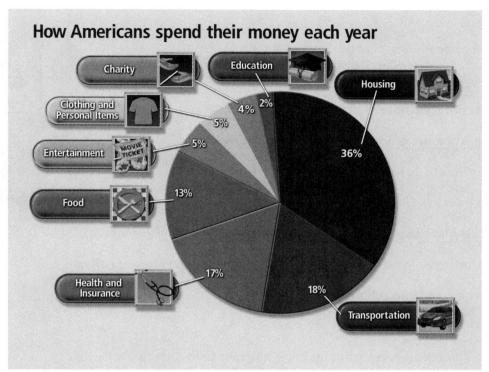

**How Americans spend their money each year**

http://www.bls.gov/opub/focus/volume2_number12/cex_2_12.htm

1. _Although_ OR _Even though_ OR _Though_ Americans spend _36_ percent of their money on housing, only 60 percent of that money is for rent or mortgage payment. The rest is spent on things like heating and cooling the home.

2. _____ Americans spend _____ percent of their money on transportation, only 34 percent of that money is for the price of a car. The rest is for gas or other kinds of transportation, like buses.

3. Health and insurance are inexpensive in other countries, _____ Americans spend _____ percent of their money on health and insurance.

4. _____ Americans spend _____ percent of their money on food, about half of that money is not spent on groceries, but instead on eating out.

5. _____ they shop, both in stores and online, Americans spend _____ percent of their money on clothing and personal items.

6. We can probably consider Americans fairly generous _____ they give _____ percent of their money to charities.

# Reducing Adverb Clauses

**1** Read the article about personal shoppers. Then rewrite the clauses in bold as reduced clauses.

Christina is a personal shopper who works for a businesswoman, Mrs. Adams. ~~Because she is very busy~~ *Being very busy*, Mrs. Adams does not have time to shop. Christina does most of her shopping. **Since she is a successful businesswoman**,

5  Mrs. Adams often has to go to events. Christina picks out dresses and shoes for her. Christina also gets groceries for Mrs. Adams. **While she gets Mrs. Adams groceries**, Christina also does her own shopping. Christina started working for Mrs. Adams **after she started college**. **Because she has earned enough money for her tuition**, Christina will finish school

10  this year.

David is also a personal shopper, but his job is different from Christina's. David goes shopping for elderly people. **Because they are homebound**, his clients have difficulty leaving their houses. David does their grocery shopping and also buys other items for them. One of his clients, Mr. Morton, said that David has changed his life.

15  **Since he had a stroke two years ago**, Mr. Morton has had trouble walking. His children did his shopping for him **before they realized a service could do it**. Now when they visit their father, they can spend time with him instead of doing errands for him.

**2** Rewrite the sentences. Use reduced clauses.

1. Because she is a "shoe addict," Melissa buys more shoes than she needs.

   *Being a "shoe addict," Melissa buys more shoes than she needs.*

2. Because she had bought 100 pairs of shoes, she didn't have room for them in her closet.

   _____

3. While she was shopping for a gift for her sister, she bought three new pairs of shoes.

   _____

4. She started buying shoes before she got a job.

   _____

5. Because they are caring people, her parents were worried about her.

_____

6. Because he had read an article about shopping addicts, her father suggested treatment.

_____

7. Melissa agreed to get help after she realized she had a problem.

_____

8. Now she takes only the money she needs when she goes to the mall.

_____

**3** Write sentences about your own shopping habits, preferences, or experiences for each topic. Use reduced clauses with information that is true for you.

1. (malls) _____ .

2. (shoes) _____ .

3. (gifts) _____ .

4. (online shopping) _____ .

5. (clothes) _____ .

# Subordinators to Express Purpose

**1** Complete the conversations. Circle the correct subordinators.

**A** **Yae Won:** Hi, Aaron. What are you doing at the mall?

**Aaron:** I need a new suit **in order to** /**so that** I can look professional for my job
(1)
interview. What are you doing here?

**Yae Won:** I came here **so** / **to** get a birthday present for my sister.
(2)

**B** **Franco:** Hey, Paul, did you ever buy that thing you needed **so that** / **to** fix your lamp?
(3)

**Paul:** No. It was almost as expensive as a new lamp! I bought a new lamp instead

**in order to** / **so** I don't have to deal with fixing it.
(4)

**C**  **Isabel:** Can you believe Doug bought a new car? He's always buying things

**in order to / so that** feel important.
(5)

**Ahmed:** Well, some people buy new things **so that / to** they can feel good. But I don't
(6)

think that's the case with Doug.

**D**  **Nina:** I have too much stuff! I'm having a sale **in order to / so** I can get rid of some of
(7)

my things. Do you want to help me?

**Vicky:** OK. But are you sure you aren't selling your stuff **so that / to** buy new things?
(8)

**2** Look at the chart about what people buy and why. Then write sentences with the
information in the chart and the words in parentheses.

| Who | Purchase | Why |
|---|---|---|
| 1.  Melissa | shoes | It makes her feel good. |
| 2.  Santiago | old guitars | He can fix them. |
| 3.  Dae Jin and Alex | concert tickets | They want to sell them to their friends. |
| 4.  Gabriela | new clothes | She can have the latest style. |
| 5.  Chuck | comic books | He likes to add them to his collection. |
| 6.  Sofia and Ying | art supplies | They can make birthday cards to sell. |

1. (in order to) _Melissa buys shoes in order to feel good._

2. (so that) _____

3. (to) _____

4. (so) _____

5. (in order to) _____

6. (so that) _____

**3** Write sentences about the reason why you buy each type of item. Use subordinators with
the words in parentheses. Write sentences that are true for you.

1. (electronics) _____

2. (books) _____

3. (gifts) _____

4. (music) _____

# Avoid Common Mistakes

**1** Circle the mistakes.

1. **Although** it's a holiday, the stores are open. **Even though** it is almost 10:00 p.m., I'm
   (a)                                                (b)
   still shopping. I'll buy something for myself, (**eventhough**) I need to get my sister a gift.
                                                     (c)

2. We're going shopping **because** I need a suit. I need you to help me. **Because** I don't
                          (a)                                              (b)
   know what looks good. **Because** I don't have a lot of money, I need to find something
                          (c)
   on sale.

3. Americans spend more on health care than Canadians **because** Canada's government
                                                        (a)
   provides more coverage. **Being** Canadian, I prefer our health care system. After **get**
                            (b)                                                        (c)
   sick last year, I didn't have to pay for any of my doctor's appointments.

4. I hate shopping **even** I like to have new clothes. I really dislike shopping alone, **although**
                    (a)                                                                   (b)
   it's sometimes easier than shopping with friends. However, I have to go shopping by
   myself tomorrow **even though** I hate it.
                    (c)

5. I'm going to buy a guitar **so that** I can play in my brother's band. I'm going to take guitar
                              (a)
   lessons **eventhough** I'm already pretty good. **Though** I don't sing that much, I might
           (b)                                      (c)
   sing backup in the band.

6. **Because** I don't want to spend money at a restaurant, I take my lunch to work. I do,
   (a)
   however, go out to eat **when** my boss pays for lunch. She takes us out every month.
                           (b)
   **Although** the restaurants are expensive.
   (c)

7. I like to shop online **even though** I can't try the clothes on. Clothing online can be
                          (a)
   cheap, **though** I have to remember to pay my credit card bill later. **Even** I have to pay
          (b)                                                              (c)
   for shipping, I usually spend less money online than in stores.

8. My roommate and I like shopping online while **watch** TV. I don't buy a lot of things,
                                                 (a)
   whereas my roommate **is** a shopping addict. After **realizing** he had a problem, he tried
                        (b)                             (c)
   to stop, but he got really depressed. I think he needs to seek professional help.

**2** Find and correct nine more mistakes in the article about spending patterns.

**Spending Patterns**

*Even though*

~~Even~~ everyone spends money differently, research shows there is a common pattern of

spending over a lifetime:

- From ages 18 to 22, people do not spend a lot of money. Young people often do not

    have a lot of money to spend. Because they are in school or getting their first job.

5 • People who are 22 to 30 spend a little more money. Although they still do not spend

    that much. For example, people in their 20s often cannot afford to buy houses when

    not earn a lot of money. As a result, they tend to rent apartments.

- From ages 31 to 40, people spend more money. They usually have more money to

    spend. Because they have been working for a while. However, eventhough they

10    make more money, they often have a hard time *saving* money.

- Research shows that people in their 40s spend the most money. Many people in this

    age group have children, so they have to buy things for the entire family.

- People in their 50s spend less money than those in their 40s even they often have

    more money than when they were younger. One of the reasons is that, eventhough

15    they may continue working, they are often trying to save money for retirement.

- People over 60 spend the least amount of money. Many people in this age group are

    not working anymore after have retired, so they are usually afraid of spending much

    money, even they have saved money for most of their lives.

# Self-Assessment

Circle the word or phrase that correctly completes each sentence.

1. You save money on sale items _____ you get a discount.

    a. while       b. because       c. although

2. _____ he was in class, Bryan was shopping online.

    a. So       b. So that       c. While

3. _____ some shoppers save on each sale item, they buy more items than they need.

   a. To     b. Although     c. In order to

4. Tatiana doesn't mind paying full price, _____ Ivan won't buy anything if it's not on sale.

   a. while     b. as     c. since

5. Some people actually spend more money _____ they use coupons.

   a. so that     b. since     c. when

6. I was shopping online before _____ my boss was near my desk.

   a. had realized     b. realize     c. realizing

7. _____ gotten a warning, Ari stopped shopping online at work.

   a. Having     b. Being     c. Because

8. _____ a teenager, Jordan spends most of her money on clothing and entertainment.

   a. Having     b. Being     c. Because

9. While _____ , Julia was sending text messages.

   a. shopping     b. shop     c. was shopping

10. Having _____ a large phone bill, Colin's parents took his phone away.

    a. get     b. gotten     c. getting

11. Katia gave away some of her old clothes after _____ new ones.

    a. to buy     b. bought     c. buying

12. I want to buy a car _____ I don't have take the bus anymore.

    a. to     b. in order to     c. so

13. Jared usually pays for dinner _____ be generous to his friends.

    a. so     b. in order to     c. so that

14. Let's go to the new Korean restaurant early so that _____ a seat.

    a. getting     b. we can get     c. get

15. I'm going to the mall to _____ a new pair of shoes.

    a. buy     b. I buy     c. buying

# Connecting Information with Prepositions and Transitions

## Technology in Entertainment

---

## Connecting Information with Prepositions and Prepositional Phrases

**1** Complete the article about acting and motion capture technology. Circle the correct prepositions and prepositional phrases.

Acting may be getting more challenging for actors **(due to)** / **besides** technology. **Instead of / Because of**

(1)                                              (2)

new inventions, actors need to find new methods of

acting. With motion capture (mocap) technology, the

actors' movements are captured and then turned into an

animation. **As well as / Instead of** wearing a tight suit

(3)

that captures movement, actors in motion capture films

may also wear a helmet[1] with a camera. **Instead of / Except for** acting on a realistic

(4)

set, actors act in a strange, empty room that may not have anything **due to / except for**

(5)

a large screen. These are challenges because actors often say sets and costumes help

them "become" a character. **In addition to / In spite of** these challenges, an actor may

(6)

sometimes talk to a spot on the screen **instead of / despite** another character. The

(7)

character that the actor is talking to will be created later by an animator. For example,

in the final movie, it may look like the actor is talking to an animated cat or a dog.

**Despite / As well as** the difficulties of acting with mocap technology, actors are doing

(8)

amazing work with it. The movies seem believable **in spite of / in addition to** the

(9)

unrealistic situations in which the actors perform.

---

[1]**helmet:** a hard hat that covers and protects the head

**2** Read the conversation about going to the movies. Then complete the sentences with the words in parentheses and information from the conversation. Sometimes more than one answer is possible.

**Martin:** Was the movie worth seeing?

**Kala:** Yes, but the ticket price was high!

**Martin:** Did you see an animated movie?

**Kala:** No. I went to an action movie.

5 **Martin:** Did you get any popcorn?

**Kala:** Yes. I'm on a diet, but I got popcorn anyway.

**Martin:** Did you get anything else?

**Kala:** Yes! I had a soda and some chocolate!

**Martin:** Did you have a good time?

10 **Kala:** Well, kind of. I couldn't see the movie very well. The theater had bad seats.

**Martin:** Is that why you're holding your neck?

**Kala:** Yes! I sat too close to the screen and now my neck hurts.

1. Kala thinks the movie was worth seeing _despite the high ticket price_
   OR _despite the ticket price being high_____ (despite).

2. Kala went to an action movie _____ (instead of).

3. Kala got popcorn _____ (in spite of).

4. Kala had a soda _____ (as well as).

5. Kala couldn't see the movie very well _____ (due to).

6. Kala's neck hurts _____ (as a result of).

**3** Combine the sentences about an animated movie. Use the prepositions in parentheses. Sometimes more than one answer is possible.

1. Let's see an animated movie. I don't want to see an action movie. (instead of)

   _Let's see an animated movie instead of an action movie._ OR _Let's see_____
   _an animated movie instead of seeing an action movie._____

2. All the movies I own are live action. *Hop* is the only animated movie I have. (except for)

   _____

3. *Hop* is a sweet movie. It's also very funny. (besides)

   _____

4. *Hop* has animated characters in it. It also has "real" actors in it. (in addition to)

_____

5. The main actor talks to other people. He also talks to an animated bunny. (as well as)

_____

**4** Write sentences about the topics in parentheses. Use the prepositions in the box or your own ideas. Write sentences that are true for you.

| as a result of | besides | except for | instead of |
| because of | despite | in addition to | |

1. (animated movies) _____

2. (action movies) _____

3. (movie ticket prices) _____

4. (movie snacks) _____

5. (mocap technology) _____

6. (renting DVDs) _____

# Connecting Information with Transition Words

**1** Look at the time line about animated movies. Then write sentences with the simple past and the sequence words in the box. Sometimes more than one answer is possible.

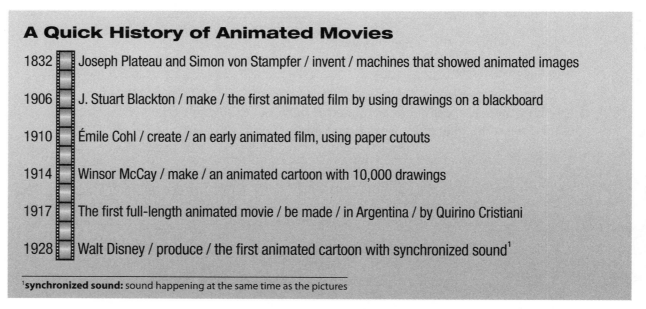

**A Quick History of Animated Movies**

1832 — Joseph Plateau and Simon von Stampfer / invent / machines that showed animated images

1906 — J. Stuart Blackton / make / the first animated film by using drawings on a blackboard

1910 — Émile Cohl / create / an early animated film, using paper cutouts

1914 — Winsor McCay / make / an animated cartoon with 10,000 drawings

1917 — The first full-length animated movie / be made / in Argentina / by Quirino Cristiani

1928 — Walt Disney / produce / the first animated cartoon with synchronized sound[1]

[1]**synchronized sound:** sound happening at the same time as the pictures

| after that | finally | ~~first~~ | next | second | then |
|---|---|---|---|---|---|

1. _First, Joseph Plateau and Simon von Stampfer invented machines_
   _that showed animated images._

2. _____

3. _____

4. _____

5. _____

6. _____

**2** Complete the paragraphs about motion capture on smartphones. Circle two transition words that correctly complete each sentence.

Motion capture (mocap) technology is used for many smartphone applications. For example, mocap is used to record people dancing. **(Then)**/ **Thus** /**(After that)**, the
(1)
movements are animated. When you use the application on your phone, you watch the animated character in order to learn the dance steps. **In addition / Moreover / Finally**,
(2)
mocap is used for exercise programs. Mocap captures people doing different kinds of exercise moves, which are turned into animation. **Instead / As a result / Consequently**,
(3)
the movements of the characters are realistic. You watch the characters on your phone and follow the exercises. The exercise program is portable when it's on your phone;
**therefore / as a result / next**, you can do the exercises anywhere at all in your home.
(4)
**Instead / Moreover / Furthermore**, you can do them when you travel.
(5)
   **In contrast / Thus / On the other hand**, some applications actually allow you to
(6)
record images using mocap. You record images easily with your phone's video camera and transfer the data to a computer. One of the uses of this application is for science experiments. For example, you can use mocap to measure movements of a moving object, like a car or an elevator. **In addition / To conclude / Furthermore**, mocap can be used
(7)
to capture movements for animation. You record movements of a person or an object with your phone's video camera.

   **On the other hand / To summarize / In conclusion**, mocap technology is now used
(8)
in a variety of smartphone apps. If they seem useful to you, get more information on them.

**3** Rewrite the sentences about a dance application (app) for a smartphone. Make each sentence into two independent sentences. Replace each word in bold with the correct transition word in parentheses.

1. U-Dance is easy to use, **and** it's a lot of fun. (also / for instance)

    *U-Dance is easy to use. Also, it's a lot of fun.*

2. Most dance apps only show steps, **but** U-Dance shows a user's movements. (to conclude / in contrast)

    _____

3. I thought the app would not be good exercise, **but** I got a good workout. (however / thus)

    _____

4. U-Dance is free, **so** you have no reason not to get it. (on the other hand / therefore)

    _____

5. **Because** it's easy to use, fun, and free, it's a great app. (to summarize / however)

    _____

# Avoid Common Mistakes

**1** Circle the mistakes.

1. I like exercising at home **as well as taking classes**. I watch exercise videos
    <sub>(a)</sub>
    (**in addition to I watch yoga videos.**) **Despite being hard work**, exercising is fun.
    <sub>(b)</sub>                            <sub>(c)</sub>

2. My sister and I enjoy TV shows. **In the other hand**, we also enjoy animated movies.
    <sub>(a)</sub>
    We see many movies at the Great Escapes Theater **as well as the Main Theater**.
    <sub>(b)</sub>
    **Despite its large size**, the Main Theater is usually very crowded.
    <sub>(c)</sub>

3. I bought a mocap application for my phone **as well as software** to make
    <sub>(a)</sub>
    animation for my computer. I recorded my son **in addition to my daughter**.
    <sub>(b)</sub>
    **In addition to my son has a cute animated character**, my daughter's animated
    <sub>(c)</sub>
    character was also cute.

4. Draw, Inc., uses traditional animation, with drawings by hand. **In contrast**, S&S Design
    <sub>(a)</sub>
    uses mocap images to animate. Draw, Inc.'s characters have more detail than S&S
    Design's. **In the other hand**, they aren't as realistic. S&S makes movies very quickly.
    <sub>(b)</sub>
    **However**, it takes Draw, Inc., a long time to make a movie.
    <sub>(c)</sub>

5. Roberto likes action movies **in addition to animated movies**. He goes to the movies
(a)

on Saturday **as well as he goes on Sunday**. He usually buys popcorn and candy
(b)

**despite the high price**.
(c)

6. Donna bought complicated animation software. **As a result**, she doesn't know how to
(a)

use it. **In the other hand**, the less complicated software didn't have the features she
(b)

wanted. **In conclusion**, Donna bought software she can't use.
(c)

7. **In addition to** the movie, the play *The Phenom Team* has a lot of action and excitement.
(a)

**In the other hand**, the play doesn't have as many special effects. I've seen the movie
(b)

**as well as** the play.
(c)

8. I'm taking an animation class **in spite of the expense**. **Despite his fast speech**, the
(a)                                  (b)

teacher is very good. He has a good sense of humor **in addition to he has patience**.
(c)

**2** Find and correct five more mistakes in the article about Pixar.

---

### Pixar: A Computer Animation Studio

*being*

Despite ~~it is~~ a relatively young company, Pixar has been very successful. In spite of

he had a good job at Disney, John Lasseter left his job to start a computer animation

company with George Lucas in 1984. The company later became Pixar. In 1986, Pixar

released its first animated short film, which was called *Luxo Jr.* In 1987, *Luxo Jr.* was

5 nominated for an Academy Award as well as it was nominated for a Golden Gate Award.

It won the Golden Gate Award. In the other hand, it did not win the Academy Award. In

1989, Pixar started making commercials in addition to it made films. In the 1990s, Pixar

continued making short films as well as it made commercials. In addition to Pixar's short

films, the commercials also won awards.

10    In 1995, Pixar's *Toy Story* was a huge success at the box office. In addition, it was the

world's first full-length movie completely animated on computers. In the years to come,

Pixar made *Toy Story 2* and *Toy Story 3*. *Toy Story 3* made even more money than the very

successful *Toy Story* and *Toy Story 2* combined. In conclusion, Pixar has had fantastic

success with many of its movies and commercials and has won a large number of awards

15 over the years.

---

# Self-Assessment

Circle the word or phrase that correctly completes each sentence.

1. Animated movies have animated characters _____ actors.

   a. in spite of      b. despite      c. instead of

2. Some movies have animated characters _____ actors.

   a. due to      b. as well as      c. because of

3. _____ using new types of computer animation, moviemakers are making some complex movie projects possible.

   a. As a result of      b. In spite of      c. Except for

4. I don't like any of the *Toy Story* movies _____ the 3D version of *Toy Story 2*.

   a. in spite of      b. because of      c. except for

5. I love going to animated movies _____ all the loud children in the audience.

   a. besides      b. as well as      c. despite

6. _____ Alejandra uses a computer program with mocap for physical therapy.

   a. Instead of using a trainer,      b. Instead using a trainer      c. Using a trainer instead of

7. The success of physical therapy programs that use mocap is _____ the realistic movements of the animation.

   a. in spite of      b. due to      c. besides

8. Paul has had success with his exercise program. _____ trouble being motivated.

   a. Other people      b. However other      c. Other people,
      however have         people have            however, have

9. First, turn on the video camera on your phone. _____ , record a moving image. After that, transfer the data to your computer.

   a. Second      b. Finally      c. Therefore

10. Carl is good at drawing. _____ , he doesn't know much about drawing on computers.

    a. Moreover      b. Instead      c. However

11. Tak-Chung works for a computer animation company; _____ , she is its artistic director.

    a. furthermore      b. on the other hand      c. then

12. Stephanie animated two short films last year. _____ , she animated four commercials.

    a. In conclusion      b. Therefore      c. In addition

13. Pixar has created several animated movies that made a lot of money, and their movies have won several awards. _____ , it's a well-known company.

    a. In contrast    b. Consequently    c. Next

14. Mocap technology is used in exercise videos; _____ , the technology is used in pilot training videos.

    a. first    b. moreover    c. thus

15. Joe's company produces some of the best computer-generated animations. Their work is _____ one of the most expensive.

    a. also    b. in addition    c. though